WHEN PRISONERS RETURN

*Why We
Should Care
and How
You and
Your Church
Can Help*

PAT NOLAN

FOREWORD BY CHUCK COLSON

PRISON
FELLOWSHIP®

When Prisoners Return
by Pat Nolan

Printed in the United States of America

ISBN 1-594676-09-7

Cover Painting: Rembrandt van Rijn, The Return of the Prodigal Son, 1668-1669. Photo © Scala /Art Resource, NY.

www.prisonfellowship.org

Dedication

To my wife, Gail, whose love and hard work held our family together during my imprisonment, and made my homecoming so joyful.

Acknowledgements

I wish to thank the following people who provided tremendous help to me on this book project:

Kim Robbins, my colleague at the Wilberforce Forum, who joyfully undertook organizing each chapter's resource guide from the snippets of information I provided her.

Mike Snyder, Sr. Vice-President of Prison Fellowship, who enthusiastically encouraged this project from beginning to end and at every step along the way.

Gene Guerrero, of the Open Society Institute, whose steady and forceful leadership on issues surrounding prisoner reentry is truly without equal.

Becky Beane, Senior Editor for Prison Fellowship, who edited my manuscript with kindness, bringing clarity and pithiness to my prose.

John Graff, Manager of Operations for Justice Fellowship, whose hard work, broad experience, brilliant insights and cheery disposition have added so much to this book and our ministry.

Pat Nolan
Leesburg, Virginia

Table of Contents

Foreword

by Chuck Colson

We live in a nation that enjoys unprecedented prosperity and power. We have access to comforts and benefits previous generations never dreamed possible.

At the same time, more than 2 million Americans are in prison, and nearly 4.5 million others are on parole. Worse yet, two-thirds of those released from prison will be in trouble with the law again within three years. For close to 30 years, Prison Fellowship has sought to reverse this revolving door of crime by discipling inmates inside the prison walls and connecting them with churches and mentors upon their release.

Now, a significant voice has joined in this effort to transform prisoners' lives. In his 2004 State of the Union address, President Bush surprised the Congress and the country by calling for a major reentry program to help offenders return to society: "America is the land of second chance, and when the gates of the prison open, the path ahead should lead to a better life."

More than 600,000 inmates will be released from America's prisons this year. To get a sense of that, realize it is three times the size of the U.S. Marine Corps—and maybe just as lethal, for in prison most inmates get a postgraduate course in crime. As the president pointed out, "We know from long experience that if they can't find work, or a home, or help, they are much more likely to commit crime and return to prison."

When inmates arrive at the front gate to be released, they're often given as little as $100, an old suit of clothes, a bus ticket home, and the guard says, "See ya in a month." For two out of three released inmates that is prophetic. And it is bad for our communities.

Remember, these men and women are coming back to our neighborhoods. The only question is the one the president asked—what's being done to prepare them to return safely and successfully to our communities? Today the answer is virtually nothing. That means more crime, more victims, and more costly prisons.

Something is clearly wrong with the whole system. What can Christians do? In this book, my colleague Pat Nolan sets out a blueprint for how the Church can join in this effort to restore peace, or *shalom*, to our neighborhoods by welcoming our brothers and sisters home, holding them accountable for their actions, and helping them become healthy, productive, law-abiding members of the community.

Pat brings a wealth of experience to this book. For 15 years he served in the California State Assembly—four of them as the Assembly Republican Leader. Then he was targeted for prosecution for a campaign contribution he received as part of a FBI sting. Pat pleaded guilty to one count of racketeering and served 25 months in a federal prison and four months in a halfway house. While Pat was in prison, my friend, Ed Meese, who had been Ronald Reagan's attorney general, suggested that I get to know Pat. He and I corresponded, and then we met at a rally where I spoke and Pat, still an inmate, gave his testimony.

After Pat's release, we asked him to run Justice Fellowship®, the criminal justice arm of Prison Fellowship. Isn't it remarkable how God has knit together these divergent experiences —prison and politics—to prepare Pat for his strategic work at Prison Fellowship?

Through the times Pat and I spent in prison, we each came to see that the American criminal justice system has proven to be a failure for one major reason: We don't understand the true nature of crime and justice. Crime is, at its root, as professors James Q. Wilson and Richard J. Herrnstein discovered in a landmark 1985 study[1], a moral problem. Inmates make wrong choices, and should be equipped to make better decisions in the future. Yet the system does little to change the moral outlook of offenders and presumes that most will reoffend and return to prison.

This doesn't have to be the case. In this book, Pat lays out the case for why the Church has an essential role in breaking the cycle of crime, and offers resources on how you and your church can help prisoners return to society safely and successfully. I hope you will join us in this important work.

---

[1] James Q. Wilson and Richard J. Herrnstein, *Crime and Human Nature* (New York: Simon & Schuster), 1985

Introduction

When President Bush called on the nation to assist released prisoners as they make the difficult transition back to their communities, he highlighted a critical need in our country. The fact that he included the Prisoner Reentry Initiative in his State of the Union address shows the importance that the president places on this issue.

For the Prisoner Reentry Initiative to be successful, we need much more than government programs. As the president said recently, "Governments can hand out money. But governments cannot put love in a person's heart, or a sense of purpose in a person's life. The truth of the matter is that comes when a loving citizen puts their arm around a brother and sister in need and says, I love you, and God loves you, and together we can perform miracles."

This is one of the roles the Church is called upon to take in our communities: to minister to the least of these. This book is intended to explain why you and your church should become involved in helping returning prisoners, and to provide you with practical ways to help.

Prison Fellowship believes that God is raising up many of the next generation of Church and community leaders from behind prison bars. Why? Because when many offenders go to prison, they hit rock bottom. They truly feel like "the least, the last, and the lost" (Matthew 25:40). They *know* they have sinned. They *know* they are unworthy of Christ's love and forgiveness. They *know* His salvation is an incredible gift. And out of deepest gratitude and humility, they surrender their lives to Him wholeheartedly. And that is when God begins to work mightily, building them into strong disciples of Christ and productive citizens. With encouragement, support, and practical assistance, many will return to society as beacons of light and hope.

But the Church's help is essential for this vision to become reality. As I emphasize elsewhere in this book, crime is, at its root, a moral and spiritual problem, and breaking free of criminal attitudes and behaviors requires a spiritual transformation. A *church-based* ministry for prisoners returning to the community is unique because the heart of its message is the Person of Jesus Christ and His power to transform lives from the inside out! Out of new life in Christ flows Christ-centered values, freedom from addiction, commitment to work, respect for authority, personal responsibility, and family reconciliation.

As the Church comes alongside returning prisoners, we can help provide or link them with valuable practical resources to get back on their feet. But most important, the Church can manifest the love of Christ to these ex-prisoners and help them become ambassadors for Christ who are grounded in God's Word, dependent on prayer, anchored in the local church, experiencing freedom from destructive habits, and living out the calling to be salt and light in their families and communities.

In support of local churches that desire to assist ex-prisoners in their community, Prison Fellowship has drawn upon nearly 30 years of experience in prison ministry to develop valuable aftercare resources. Prison Fellowship can provide:

- Extensive **training** to help churches set up a strategy that is customized to the needs and resources of their particular congregation and community;
- A **basic familiarity** with prison life, ex-prisoners'

needs and attitudes, and the workings of the criminal justice system;

- **Teaching materials** designed especially for ex-prisoners that will help them "make it" on the outside;
- Ongoing **support services** as the churches' ministries change and grow.

Prison Fellowship has several local "hub" offices strategically placed throughout the United States to assist churches in the surrounding area. To find out more about specific training opportunities and resources, we encourage you to contact the hub office nearest you. To receive this contact information:

- Call toll-free (877) 478-0100 and ask for the phone number of the office in your area.
- Visit www.prisonfellowship.org. Click on "local offices" and follow the directions to contact the nearest hub office.
- Write to the Prison Fellowship National Office at P.O. Box 1550, Merrifield, VA 22116-1550.

In addition to Prison Fellowship's Aftercare efforts, many other ministries, churches, community organizations and programs have long been serving returning inmates. Their depth of experience and materials can provide valuable guidance to you and your church as you set up a ministry to ex-prisoners. We encourage you to take advantage of the wealth of resources listed in this book. We invite you to join God as He raises up disciples and leaders from among "the least of these."

In His service,
Pat Nolan
Leesburg, Virginia

CHAPTER 1

600,000 Offenders Returning Home—Who Cares?

"We know from long experience that if they can't find work, or a home, or help, they are much more likely to commit more crimes and return to prison."
—*President Bush, State of the Union 2004*

More than 600,000 inmates will be released from America's prisons this year, having finished their sentences. That is over 1,600 offenders per day returning to neighborhoods across the country. These men and women are coming out, like it or not.

What kind of neighbors will these returning inmates be? What has been done to prepare them to live healthy, productive, law-abiding lives? Each of us has a stake in seeing that these men and women make a safe and successful return to their communities. Yet, today very little is being done to help them make that transition.

Most offenders will be returning from years in overcrowded prisons where they were exposed to the horrors of violence—including homosexual rape—isolation from family and friends, and despair. Most were idle in prison, warehoused with little preparation to make better choices

1

when they return to the free world. Just one-third of all released prisoners will have received vocational or educational training in prison.

The number of prisoners released is now four times what it was 20 years ago, yet fewer are being prepared to return to their communities. While approximately three of every four inmates released from prison have a substance abuse problem, only one in five has received drug treatment.

These men and women face additional barriers, often called "invisible punishments": They are frequently denied parental rights, driver's licenses, student loans, the right to vote, and residency in public housing—which is often the only housing that they can afford.

Further, little is done to change the moral perspective of offenders. Most inmates do not leave prison transformed into law-abiding citizens; in fact, the very skills inmates develop to survive inside prison make them anti-social when they are released. Most are given a bus ticket to their hometown, gate money of between $20 and $200, and infrequently a new set of clothes. Upon leaving prison they will have great difficulty finding employment.

If we do not prepare these inmates for their return to the community, the odds are great that their first incarceration will not be their last. The statistics tell the story. A recent study by the Bureau of Justice Statistics found that two out of three released inmates were rearrested within three years, victimizing more innocents in the process. Over the last 30 years, the rate of rearrest has hovered stubbornly around 67 percent.

As the number of people released from prison and jail increases steadily, we cannot afford to continue to send them home with little preparation. These policies have harmed too many victims, destroyed too many families, overwhelmed too many communities, and wasted too many lives as they repeat the cycle of arrest, incarceration, release and rearrest. The toll this system takes is not measured merely in human lives: The strain on taxpayers has been tremendous. As jail and prison populations have soared, so have corrections budgets, creating fiscal crises in virtually every state and squeezing money for schools, health care, and roads from state budgets.

It does not have to be this way. Fortunately, there are proven ways to increase the likelihood that inmates will return safely to our communities. There are many things that the community, and particularly churches, can do to help offenders make the transition from prison life to freedom successfully.

One of the most important ways to help is to mentor a returning prisoner. These men and women need relationships with loving, moral people far more than they need any program. Government programs can't love them; only people can do that. Dr. Martin Luther King, Jr., said, "To change someone, you must first love them, and they must know that you love them."

One crucial way mentors show their love to returning inmates is to "meet them at the gate," walking with them as they take those first difficult steps in freedom. As they move from the very structured environment of prison, in which they had virtually no control over any aspect of their lives, their return to their community presents them with a myriad of options and temptations. Such basic decisions as where to sleep, where to seek employment, and with whom to associate confront them the minute they hit the street. As offenders make the transition back into the community, they need someone to provide love, advice, and encouragement, and to hold them accountable for their actions.

Obviously a good job is essential if these men and women are to make a successful transition from prison back to the community. Work helps support their families. It pays for rent, food, clothes, and the other necessities of life. In addition, work puts offenders into daily contact with the mainstream of the community, forming positive relationships with "everyday" people.

Being unemployed, on the other hand, leaves offenders with time on their hands and can often lead inmates into trouble. Our mothers wisely taught us that idle hands are the Devil's playground. Watching TV or hanging out with others in the neighborhood is a recipe for a return to the wrong lifestyle.

Of course, for a mentor to truly make a difference, the offenders' attitudes must be changed. At its root, crime is a spiritual and moral problem, as well as a legal problem. People go to prison as a result of bad moral choices, and their hearts must be transformed if they are to lead crime-free lives when they get out.

The world has largely given up on changing the behavior of offenders. The Church, on the other hand, believes in redemption. The Church reaches out in love, embracing the offenders while inviting them to repent of their sin and find forgiveness in Christ. The Church also knows that it is important to hold offenders accountable for the harm they have done and to challenge them to make things right with their victims, if possible. Most important, the Church calls offenders to turn their lives over to God for real transformation.

The apostle Paul's entire letter to Philemon is a request for help for a prisoner returning home. Writing from inside a prison in Rome, Paul asks his friend Philemon to welcome Philemon's former slave, Onesimus, who apparently had stolen from him and then escaped. "Perhaps the reason he was separated from you for a little while was that you might have him back for good—no longer as a slave, but better than a slave, as a dear brother. He is very dear to me but even dearer to you, both as a man and as a brother in the Lord. So if you consider me a partner, welcome him as you would welcome me. If he has done you any wrong or owes you anything, charge it to me" (Philemon 1:15-18, NIV).

Paul asked Philemon to welcome Onesimus as a brother in Christ—not as a criminal.

Onesimus had become a Christian as a result of Paul's ministry, and Paul wanted to make sure that Onesimus got a fair chance at a new life. Can we do any less for our returning brothers and sisters?

Fear of rejection by their hometown church is one of the greatest fears many Christian inmates experience as their sentence comes to a close and they prepare for their return home. This is not an irrational fear. Sadly, there are many stories of inmates who returned home with a vibrant faith, but because they had a criminal record —as well as some missing teeth and perhaps a tattoo or two—they were asked not to come back to church.

A welcoming church is crucial for returning prisoners who have become Christians in prison. To continue their new life in Christ means they must avoid many of their old friends and may even have to shun family members with alcohol or drug addictions. Where will these newly minted Christians turn for companionship and positive activities if they are rejected by their local church? The greater the density of loving, moral people we can pack around returning prisoners, the greater the chance that they will become healthy, productive, law-abiding members of the community.

Here are some important things you, your church, and your community can do to help offenders make the difficult transition back to free society:

Commit: Make a personal commitment to help these returning offenders. It could be as a mentor, employer, Bible teacher, or volunteer at a halfway house. Or perhaps you could drive offenders to a doctor's appointment, invite them out for a nice hot meal, or provide a bus pass so they can get to work. Most important, invite them to attend church with your family.

Reach Out: Speak with your pastor about the importance of helping prisoners as they return to your community, and offer to work with him or her to develop a plan for your congregation to serve them. Invite others to join you in this work. Discuss the needs of returning prisoners with members of your Bible study, service clubs, and neighbors. Write your elected officials and your local newspapers, encouraging them to support these efforts.

Survey: Find out what services are already being provided in your community. See where God is at work, and pitch in. It is a lot easier to join in work that is already being done than to start from scratch. When Prison Fellowship has surveyed community groups to determine what is being done to assist returning offenders, we have frequently found that many groups aren't even aware of the services others are providing.

Convene: One very important way your church can serve your community is to convene a meeting of these groups to learn what each is doing, find out how you can help them, and develop a plan to fill any gaps in the services ex-offenders need.

Include: Work with groups that provide housing, job placement, drug treatment, health care, and other services that returning prisoners need to make sure they include them among the clients they serve.

You and your church can be the arms of the body of Christ, reaching out to embrace His returning sons and daughters. If your church would like to develop a ministry to returning prisoners, Prison Fellowship offers training, support, and materials written from a Christian perspective. As President Bush said, "America is the land of the second chance—and when the gates of the prison open, the path ahead should lead to a better life."

Resources for this chapter can be found beginning on page 61.

CHAPTER 2

A Changed Heart

To deal effectively with crime, we must first understand it. At its root, crime is a moral problem. Offenders make bad moral choices that result in harm to their victims. To break the cycle of crime, we must address this immoral behavior. There aren't enough police officers to stop everyone tempted to do something bad from doing it; inmates must rely on inner restraint to keep from harming others. If inmates are to live healthy, productive, law-abiding lives when they return to their communities, we must equip them with moral standards to live up to and a worldview that explains why they should do so.

Job training and education alone won't transform an inmate from a criminal into a law-abiding citizen. For some inmates such programs merely make them smarter, more sophisticated criminals. It is a changed heart that can transform a prisoner into a law-abiding citizen. Unfortunately, many prison programs ignore the moral aspect of crime and avoid all discussion of faith and morality. In doing so, they are missing a significant factor that has proven effective at changing criminals' behavior: faith.

Most people assume that faith is encouraged in prison. I certainly did when I was in the legislature. Yet, when I was incarcerated I found the opposite was true. It puzzled me. I had assumed that wardens, even if they were atheists, would encourage inmates to be involved in religious activities. After all, if you were a corrections officer and you saw a group of inmates coming across the yard, wouldn't it make a difference if you knew they were coming from Bible study?

While there are many corrections officials who encourage religious involvement and welcome religious volunteers, many others do not. It is the public that loses out when faith is ignored, because several studies have documented the significant role faith can play in helping inmates turn their lives around.

One study of the impact of religion on rehabilitation found that religious programs combat the negative effects of prison culture and that religious volunteers are a largely untapped resource pool available to administer educational, vocational, and treatment services at little or no cost.

In another study, the John Templeton Foundation funded a recidivism research project by the National Institute of Healthcare Research to study data on inmates in four New York prisons. This study concluded that prisoners who attended 10 or more Prison Fellowship programs each year were 64 percent less likely to be rearrested within a year than inmates in a matched comparison group.

For years Prison Fellowship desired a way to not only share the good news of salvation with inmates, but also to disciple them in how to live out their faith after returning home. We sought an opportunity to immerse inmates in a healthy, moral environment in which they could learn their responsibilities to their victims, their spouse, their children, their employer, and their community. We wanted the chance to help prisoners apply their faith to the real-life challenges that would face them upon release from prison.

In such a program, we envisioned recruiting mentors from local churches who would establish a relationship with the prisoners inside prison and be there to walk out the prison gate with them, welcoming them back to the community and introducing them to their church, assisting them in locating employment, helping them think through the challenges of transition from prison, and holding them accountable to walk the straight path.

That is exactly what Prison Fellowship set out to do when it developed the InnerChange Freedom Initiative® (IFI), the values-based corrections program taught from a biblical perspective that was introduced in Texas in 1997 with the support of then Governor George W. Bush, and now operating in Texas, Kansas, Iowa, and Minnesota— with other states showing an interest. Our goal was to slow down recidivism—that revolving door that leads out of our prisons and then right back in again.

Participation in IFI is voluntary, and there is no time off or other incentives for inmates to participate. But those who choose to be in IFI are immersed daily in values-based teachings grounded in a biblical perspective and are required to work and improve their education. The second half of the program includes six months of community service outside the prison. While they are in prison, they are paired with mentors from local churches who work with them to understand their responsibilities to their spouses, children, and employers. The program continues after the inmates are released with ongoing guidance from mentors along with support from a local church.

IFI-Texas was the subject of a recent study by Dr. Byron Johnson of the University of Pennsylvania. The study, "The InnerChange Freedom Initiative, a Preliminary Evaluation of a Faith-Based Program," contains wonderful news for those of us who believe that inmates can turn their lives around if they are spiritually transformed on the "inside."

The study followed IFI graduates for two years after their release and compared them to inmates with similar backgrounds and offenses who had not participated in IFI. The study found that:

- InnerChange Freedom Initiative graduates were 50 percent less likely to be rearrested. The two-year post-release rearrest rate among InnerChange Freedom Initiative program graduates in Texas is 17.3 percent, compared with 35 percent of the matched comparison group.

- InnerChange Freedom Initiative graduates were 60-percent less likely to be reincarcerated. The two-year post-release reincarceration rate among InnerChange Freedom Initiative program graduates in Texas is 8 percent, compared with 20.3 percent of the matched comparison group.

These findings offer much promise to our communities. "All but one thousand of Texas's 143,000 prisoners have an eventual release date," noted Fred Becker, the first warden at IFI-Texas. "It's up to us to determine what kind of shape they come back to the world in. If we can stop only 10 percent of those inmates from re-offending, it will mean thousands of citizens who never become victims of crime. InnerChange is a step in that direction."

You don't have to be a believer to appreciate the benefits that IFI is providing to the community: fewer victims, safer neighborhoods, reduced court cases, and fewer prisoners. In a *Wall Street Journal* editorial titled "Jesus Saves," Bill McGurn wrote, ". . . critics of the faith-based approach may claim that their only issue is with religion. But if these results are any clue, increasingly the argument against such programs requires turning a blind eye to science." As Charles Colson noted, the positive outcomes that result from faith can no longer be denied.

From his interviews with the IFI participants, Johnson identified five "themes" that are associated with successful rehabilitation, each one of them a part of the IFI teaching:

- having a willingness to condemn their previous behavior;
- recognizing that life is a "work in progress" and that spiritual growth is a lifelong process;
- replacing the values of prison society with something more worthwhile;
- developing a sense of hope and purpose; and
- sensing the need to give back to society.

"Now we have hard evidence," said Prison Fellowship President Mark Earley, "that vindicates our approach to this pressing social problem: that the best way to close the revolving doors of our prisons is to open human hearts to the transforming power of the Gospel."

President Bush realizes this, and that is why he convened a meeting in the Roosevelt Room to discuss the study with Attorney General Ashcroft, Secretary of Labor Elaine Chao, Jim Towey, the director of the White House Office of Faith- Based and Community Initiatives, Charles Colson, Mark Earley, and three IFI graduates.

The president and other administration officials expressed excitement about Dr. Johnson's study. "Faith-based initiatives are about transforming lives," Towey said. "This study indicates early signs of making headway toward reducing recidivism. All of society benefits when prison inmates are transformed."

However, the president's actions as he walked into the room spoke more loudly than any words uttered that day. Walking past Colson, Earley, and members of his Cabinet and staff, the president made a beeline to Robert Sutton, an IFI graduate and a convicted murderer. Their meeting in the Roosevelt Room wasn't their first. They had met before in 1997 at the dedication of IFI-Texas, where the governor put his arm around Sutton while the inmate choir sang "Amazing Grace." The *Houston Chronicle* had run the picture of the governor on the front page with a caption noting that he was embracing a murderer.

Since then, Sutton has graduated from IFI and has made a successful transition to the free world, leading Bible studies for young people in his church. Now President Bush and Sutton were together again, this time in the White House rather than a prison. Both men beamed as they embraced— the president and a murderer, celebrating their brotherhood in Jesus Christ, both forgiven by their Savior and changed men because of it.

Resources for this chapter can be found beginning on page 69.

CHAPTER 3

A Welcoming Church and Loving Mentors

The moment offenders step off the bus, they face several critical decisions: Where will they live, where will they be able to find a meal, where should they look for a job, how will they get from one place to the next, and where can they earn enough money to pay for these necessities? These returning inmates are also confronted with many details of personal business, such as obtaining various identification cards and documents, making medical appointments, and working through the many everyday bureaucratic problems that occur during any transition. These choices prompt feelings of intense stress and worry over the logistics of their return to the outside world. To someone who has had no control over any aspect of their lives for many years, each of these problems can be vexing. In accumulation, they can be overwhelming.

My own experience provides a good example. Shortly after my release from prison to the halfway house, some friends took me to lunch at a local deli. The waiter came over to take our orders. Everyone else told him what they wanted, but I kept poring over the menu. My eyes raced over the columns of choices. I knew that I was supposed to order, but the number of options overwhelmed me. My friends sat in embarrassed silence. I was paralyzed. The waiter looked at me impatiently. I began to panic. How ridiculous that I wasn't able to do such a simple thing as order lunch. Finally, in desperation I ordered the next item my eyes landed on, a turkey sandwich. I didn't even want it, but at least it put an end to this embarrassing incident.

For two years I hadn't been allowed to make any choices about what I ate. Now I was having a hard time adjusting to the simple options most people face every day. If I had this much difficulty after only a couple of years in prison, think how hard it is for those inmates who haven't made any choices for five, ten, or fifteen years. When faced with a baffling array of options, is it any surprise that so many newly released prisoners make some bad choices and end up back in prison?

The choices offenders make immediately after release are extremely important. Of the ex-prisoners who fail (that is, are rearrested), over half will fail within the first six months. That is not much time to turn their lives around. One study of rearrests in New York City found that the rate was especially high during the first hours and days following release. This early window of time is the most intense period for ex-prisoners, when they may be overwhelmed by the accumulation of large and small decisions facing them. On average, ex-offenders have only a one-in-three chance of getting through their first three years without being arrested.

During their difficult first days on the street, returning prisoners need relationships with loving, moral adults who will help them reenter society successfully. Programs are helpful, but a program cannot love these former inmates; only people can do that. You and your church can provide these men and women with the love, encouragement, and assistance that they so desperately need.

First, you should locate agencies in your local community that work with ex-offenders, such as workforce development organizations, housing agencies, substance abuse treatment, medical and mental health clinics, and legal services. Determine the extent to which they can be of help, and refer returning inmates to them as appropriate. If there are gaps in the services available, you and your church can:

- Assist in locating affordable housing.
- Provide emergency food.
- Offer job counseling.
- Connect with a clothing bank for appropriate clothes for work.
- Assist in reuniting families where appropriate. This is particularly important for non-custodial parents.
- Provide counseling on family issues, including helping to deal with changes in relationships with family and loved ones that resulted from incarceration.
- Connect them to job training, education, and social services, and locate resources in the community to meet other needs.

It is important to make these returning brothers and sisters feel welcome in your church. After years of having every minute of their lives controlled by prison authorities, offenders return to find themselves with unending hours of unstructured time to contend with. Unless they are quickly drawn into positive activities, the temptation is to "hang" on the street corner or watch TV for hours at a time. Boredom and loneliness are twin curses that will likely lead them into bad situations.

Church activities offer a positive way to fill this time. Worship services, Bible studies, and church social groups are wholesome activities that draw the returning offenders into a "good crowd," and provide them with positive role models. Christian inmates frequently experience a deep fellowship and intense worship among the small circle of believers on the "inside." When they return to their communities they miss this closeness among their fellow congregants. I certainly missed that fellowship of believers after I left prison. (That is just about the only aspect of prison life I have longed for.)

One former addict said that quitting drugs was much easier than dropping his old friends when he got out. We all seek to belong, and if the church doesn't welcome these returning inmates, they will seek fellowship elsewhere. The church offers a positive alternative to street life for ex-offenders. Dr. John DiIulio, who was President Bush's first director of the Office of Faith Based and Community Initiatives, pointed out the stark dividing lines of urban life: "The last two institutions to leave the inner city are liquor stores and the church." Make returning inmates feel welcome in your church, and their old lives won't seem so attractive.

In addition to participating in group activities with your congregation, it is important that returning inmates have a friend they can turn to as they take their difficult first steps in freedom. A loving mentor can help them think through their decisions and hold them accountable for making the right moral choices. Being a mentor to a returning inmate is the greatest demonstration of love you can give them.

The importance of mentors to returning prisoners was stressed by Dr. Byron Johnson in his recent study of the Texas InnerChange Freedom Initiative (IFI), the reentry program operated by Prison Fellowship under contract with the state. Dr. Johnson's study found that IFI graduates were two and a half times less likely to be reincarcerated than inmates in a control group. The two-year post-release reincarceration rate among IFI graduates in Texas was 8 percent, compared with 20.3 percent of the matched comparison group.

Dr. Johnson emphasized that mentors were "absolutely critical" to the impressive results. The support and accountability provided by mentors often make the difference between a successful return to society and re-offending. As these offenders make the difficult transition back into the community, they need relationships with caring, moral adults. The greater the density of good people we pack around them, the greater the chance that they will be successfully replanted into the community.

A mentor can help the ex-offenders think through employment options and tell them what their employer will expect of them on the job. Many offenders have never had someone in their lives who has held a steady job. They have no model for being a good employee. A mentor can teach them that they need to get up on time, go to work each day, and call their supervisor if they must be late or absent. Offenders may find it difficult to take direction or may lack skills to cope with a difficult boss or fellow employees. A mentor can help them with these and other everyday difficulties of the workplace and teach them the importance of punctuality, politeness, and diplomacy on the job.

Mentors can also help the offenders learn decision-making skills and teach them how to keep track of bills and pay them on time. In prison, inmates do not have to deal with any of this. On the street such details may quickly overwhelm them. In short, offenders need to be taught how to make good choices, handle responsibility, and be accountable—to make the right choice even when no one is looking.

Mentors also help returning inmates deal with many of the personal problems they typically encounter upon leaving prison: no reliable friends outside their former gang network, marital problems, and no easy way to get on with life. While mentors provide a much-needed emotional safety net for returning felons, they should not taken in by "poor me" stories. As one mentor said, "When a guy tells me his boss is mean or that his sister is going to kick him out of her house if he doesn't get a job, I tell him to deal with it. I point out that he has made a lot of mistakes and that he's going to have to do whatever it takes to change his life."

Some practical ways a mentor can help ex-offenders:

- Assist them in developing a "life plan."
- Identify their strengths and weaknesses, skills and abilities so that they can find employment that is tailored to those qualities.
- Coach them in job interview skills.
- Help them write their résumé and fill out job applications.
- Provide them with a ride or a bus pass to get to job interviews and job searches.
- When they locate a job, introduce yourself to their supervisor and offer to help when issues arise.
- Introduce them to your congregation and include them in your worship services, Bible studies, and other activities and support services.
- Help them develop independent living skills, such as budgeting or shopping.
- Help them deal with difficulties with their family and loved ones.
- Meet their parole or probation officer, and make sure they keep their appointments. Let the supervising authorities know you are available to help as issues arise.
- Drive them to parole or probation appointments, if necessary.
- Accompany them to medical and social service appointments to help them tolerate delays in waiting rooms and other challenges.
- Be available to help when temptation arises.

Ideally, the relationship between mentors and offenders should begin while they are still in prison. That way, they can establish rapport and think through the options for life after prison prior to their release. For prisoners who are in institutions too far away to visit, you may try using teleconferencing if the technology is available from the correctional institution. Or, if necessary, you can establish a relationship by phone calls and letters. For obvious reasons, it is important that the mentor be the same sex as the offender.

It is helpful to meet ex-offenders at the gate or bus station and to keep company with them during their first critical hours after release. A mentor provides stability and companionship at a time of acute vulnerability. Coming alongside right away can also cement the relationship between mentor and ex-prisoners at a time when it is very important to establish trust.

Most people can remember a teacher, coach, or neighbor who believed in them and helped them believe in themselves. That is exactly what returning offenders need, yet most have never had someone like that in their lives. Mentors can fill that void. A loving mentor lets returning inmates know that the community is invested in their success. You can provide the love that Paul asked Philemon to give to Onesimus: "So if you consider me a partner, welcome him as you would welcome me."

Resources for this chapter can be found beginning on page 76.

CHAPTER 4

A Safe Place to Live

"When a man or woman comes out of prison, there has to be something waiting for them other than the street, other than homelessness."
—*Hon. Jack Kemp, former Secretary of Housing and Urban Development*

The first few days after release are critical for returning prisoners. One study in New York City found that rearrests were especially high during the first hours and days following release. On average, ex-prisoners have only a one-in-three chance of getting through their first three years without being arrested. By six months post-release, a majority of those who will be arrested have been. Thus, this early period after release will have a great impact on whether the ex-offender will successfully reenter the community as a contributing, law-abiding citizen or return to prison.

The moment inmates step off the bus, a daunting challenge stares them in the face: where to find a safe place to sleep that night. Many people presume that all returning inmates are violent and that they can fend for themselves on the street. However, contrary to popular belief, the majority of offenders are not incarcerated for violent offenses, and being victimized is one of their greatest worries when they are released.

For offenders who come from good homes with loving spouses, parents or siblings, that is the best environment to which they can return. Their family already knows them, and is willing to encourage and support them in getting back on their feet.

For many returning offenders, however, this is not an option. An inmate's family may have died or moved during the incarceration, or a family may be reluctant to welcome an inmate back. There may be family conflicts, or the offender or other family members may have alcohol or drug addictions that make returning home a bad environment for the offender. Federal law poses another barrier, preventing many inmates from returning to live with families who live in public housing.

Where do those without a family member or close friend to take them in live when they are released from prison? Released prisoners are only a small portion of those competing for a very limited supply of low-cost housing. There are usually long waiting lists for the few units that become available. Offenders who have just gotten off the bus don't have the option of waiting; they need to find a place to sleep *that night*. Many end up in homeless shelters.

Recent studies in New York City found that more than 30 percent of those entering its homeless shelters had recently been released from correctional institutions. A survey of Boston shelters found that nearly one-quarter of the released prison population experienced homelessness within a year of release; some were homeless immediately upon release, while others became homeless shortly thereafter, when temporary living situations dissolved.

While homeless shelters are far better than sleeping under a bridge or in a park, they are not conducive to successful reentry for offenders. The beds are often available only at night, so residents are forced out onto the streets during the day. This time to "roam" is not good for former inmates who are used to having every minute of their day structured. The few possessions that inmates bring with them from prison, including necessary paperwork, have to be taken with them each day. By their very nature, homeless shelters are temporary, yet returning offenders need permanence, and a safe place to live is essential to re-establishing themselves in the community.

If they are fortunate enough to locate an affordable unit, it is often located away from public transit and they have no way to get there. Even if they can find a way to get to the housing, they usually have no money to pay the required first and last months' rent.

Helping ex-offenders find affordable housing is one of the most important ways the Church can help them make a safe and successful return to the community. Prison Fellowship has found that many faith-based and community groups are already providing essential services to returning prisoners. Oftentimes, however, they don't know that the others exist or what services are being provided. You should determine what groups are serving ex-prisoners and whether their efforts are being coordinated. If there is no such coordinating group, your church can provide an essential service by convening a meeting of these providers and discussing ways that you can cooperate to serve returning offenders.

You and your congregation can work with local affordable housing groups to ensure that their programs include returning offenders. Some low-cost housing agencies and homeless shelters require a period of "clean and sober living," often six months, before admitting a new resident. On the surface, this appears to be a reasonable requirement. However, returning inmates need housing immediately, not after six months. If they have no place to live for the first six months post-release, they are a lot less likely to stay clean and law-abiding.

For many inmates, the best placement is in the structured

setting of a halfway house. Some national groups such as Volunteers of America operate halfway houses in several communities. In other communities Christian families or individuals have answered the call to meet this critical need.

One such family, Manny and Barbara Mill, founded Koinonia House, a temporary home for recently released Christian prisoners —"Not a Halfway House but an All-the-Way House," says Manny. The residents live there for an average of 15 months, long enough for the former prisoner to become reintegrated into the community, gainfully employed, and linked to a church.

Manny and Barbara know the needs of ex-prisoners, because Manny himself is an ex-offender. He came from a good family and was a successful insurance broker. However, the lure of the good life drew him into a scheme to pass forged checks, and he ended up serving several years in prison.

Upon his release, Manny was determined to help those like him who had gotten into trouble but had used their time in prison to turn their lives over to Christ. "You can't teach to others what you haven't experienced yourself," he explains. Manny and Barbara set up his first house in Wheaton, Illinois, close to his alma mater, in 1991.

Manny has a vision of a national network of Koinonia Houses, each under the leadership of "discipleship and resident directors"—usually a retired Christian married couple. The couples disciple up to four male or four female recently released prisoners in the homes. "More than four," Manny explains, "and you lose the sense of a family structure, and start getting a boarding house."

In the 12 years since establishing Koinonia House, Manny and Barbara have established five houses. Chaplains refer potential residents to Manny or his staff, usually about six months before release. They visit candidates in prison and assess their need, their walk with Christ, and their desire to make a fresh start in life. Once selected, each participating offender enters into a written covenant with Koinonia House. And on the day of their release, they are met at the gate by a member of their new "family."

Most people aren't able to start a Christian halfway house like Manny and Barbara, but there are many other ways you can help, such as helping a returning offender find suitable housing, donating money or furniture to a halfway house, or working with the local housing agency to coordinate services to ex-offenders. However you and your church decide to assist ex-prisoners housing should be a priority.

" 'For I was hungry and you gave me food, I was thirsty and you gave me something to drink, I was a stranger and you invited me in, I was naked and you gave me clothing, I was sick and you took care of me, I was in prison and you visited me.' Then the righteous will answer him, 'Lord, when did we see you hungry and feed you, or thirsty and give you something to drink? When did we see you a stranger and invite you in, or naked and clothe you? When did we see you sick or in prison and visit you?' And the king will answer them, 'I tell you the truth, just as you did it for one of the least of these brothers or sisters of mine, you did it for me' " (Matthew 25:35-40).

Resources for this chapter can be found beginning on page 83.

CHAPTER 5

A Good Job

A good job is an essential element in the successful return to the community from prison. Finding a stable and adequate income upon release could well determine whether an offender makes a successful transition or not. Studies have shown that holding a legitimate job lessens the chances of re-offending. Also, the higher the wages the returning prisoners receive, the lower the odds that they will become involved in another crime.

Finding employment has a direct and positive impact on the viability and stability of ex-offenders, their families, and communities. Having a job provides ex-offenders with money to pay for rent, food, and support of their family. Jobs often include medical coverage for the worker and their family. Plus, with every paycheck, employees see that their employer values their labor so much that they get paid for it. That is a wonderful morale booster.

On the other hand, the lack of a job and paycheck causes harm in many ways. Unemployment makes the returning prisoners a financial drain on their family and often leads to resentment of those who have to contribute to their support. It leaves the ex-offenders feeling inadequate, and further lowers their feelings of self-worth, already very low as a result of their incarceration.

Work also fills the day with productive activities and

puts ex-offenders in contact with people in the mainstream of society. Idleness is destructive, particularly for former inmates, who leave the strict control of prison life to suddenly confront unending hours of unstructured time. A job gives them the structure they need and helps them stay out of trouble.

Given the key role employment plays in determining whether a prisoner's return is successful or not, it is troubling that most inmates get little or no training, and few have an actual job in place when they leave prison. In urban areas, the numbers of prisoners returning without a job are particularly sobering. For instance, of more than 400 inmates from Chicago, only 14 percent had a job lined up when they were interviewed prior to their release.

Although most prisoners held a job before their incarceration, they are confronted with many barriers to employment when they return. Some impediments are longstanding: for instance, poor job skills; low education levels; unstable family situations; histories of substance, physical, and sexual abuse; and medical and mental health issues. Other impediments result directly from their crime and imprisonment, such as lost time in the labor force and the social stigma of being an ex-con.

In addition, returning inmates face a significant number of systemic barriers to employment. Several states have laws that prevent ex-offenders from holding jobs in certain environments such as schools, nursing homes, and hospitals. Many states even exclude ex-offenders from being barbers or cosmetologists, the very skills many inmates develop inside prison. These "invisible punishments" may make sense for offenders whose criminal history would pose a threat in particular types of work, but blanket prohibitions needlessly limit the job prospects of returning inmates. Should someone who passed bad checks be prevented from cutting hair? Many offenders are released without driver's licenses or state-issued ID cards. In the post 9/11 environment, it is virtually impossible to open a bank account, rent a motel room, or board a flight without a picture ID. Identification papers are also needed to cash a check and access medical services and employment assistance. Without an ID, the ex-prisoner is stranded.

These systemic barriers are accompanied by the very real biases most employers hold against ex-offenders. Two-thirds of employers have a policy of not knowingly hiring anyone with criminal background. To the extent that such issues prevent an offender from finding a job, they also present serious risks—and lost opportunities—for the communities to which large numbers of prisoners return.

The general lack of job-placement assistance and other follow-up after release from prison is one cited reason that job training has not been more effective in reducing recidivism. This follow-up period may be particularly important for employers who indicate a willingness to hire former prisoners if a third-party intermediary or case manager is available to work with the new hire to help avert problems.

Studies show that employers are much more likely to hire inmates who are part of a structured system of oversight and monitoring. Because companies are not equipped to help inmates deal with the many non-job related problems confronting them, employers are far more willing to hire ex-offenders if they know that a system is in place to hold them accountable for their actions and help with problems that may arise.

You and your church can provide this critical link of accountability and assistance. Knowing that your church is working with the offender and is ready to assist when issues arise will greatly increase the willingness of a potential employer to hire the ex-offender. Here are some key ways you and your church can help:

Reach out to potential employers. Talk to potential employers within your congregation, as well as in service clubs or professional associations to which you belong. Let them know about the free services that are available to them: screening of prospective employees, job readiness training, and job retention services for ex-offenders. They will also be happy to learn about the Federal Bonding Program, which insures the employer against theft, forgery, larceny, or embezzlement, and the Work Opportunity Tax Credits.

Be available to assist the employer and the ex-offender. When an employer hires an ex-offender, develop a personal relationship with them by visiting the job site. Maintain a consistent follow-up and quick response to any problems that arise.

Cooperate with community and government agencies. Build the capacity of organizations that provide employment and training services to ex-offenders and their employers. Determine what programs your local community colleges offer that would help ex-offenders get jobs, including GED, Adult Education, and job-training programs. Cultivate close relationships with area probation and parole officers to affect retention rates. Cultivate relationships with area One Stop employment centers to provide ex-offenders access to job opportunities.

Listen to employers. Give them a meaningful role in influencing the shape and type of programs, services, and outcomes for your program. Employers who have had a good experience with hiring former inmates are the best source of new jobs.

Publicize success stories. Ask a local newspaper or TV station to highlight the story of a successful inmate you have helped place in a job. Make sure to emphasize the positive contributions that the ex-offender is making as a parent, soccer coach, member of the choir, or other community-related activities. Encourage local service clubs to honor former inmates who have safely and successfully made the transition back to the community.

Match each offender with a mentor from your congregation. It is important that they have a loving, moral adult who will think through the challenges of finding and maintaining a job. (See A Welcoming Church and Loving Mentors.)

Your goal should be to expand opportunities for inmates to work, learn useful skills, and earn wages, while developing a good work ethic. If these goals are met, the inmates will be able to pay restitution to anyone they have harmed, contribute to the support of their families, and develop skills that will ease their return to free society.

First, you should teach returning inmates their responsibilities as an employee. Many prisoners have never had a job that resembles anything that we would call work. And in many cases they have never lived with an adult who holds a steady job. Few inmates engage in any type of meaningful work experience or vocational education while in prison. In a 1997 survey, just over half of all soon-to-be-released prisoners had a work assignment in prison, only 35 percent had participated in educational programs, and only 27 percent had received any vocational training.

Second, teach them what their employer will expect of them: They need to show up on time, put in a day's work for a day's pay, and inform their employer if they will be absent or late. Most important, you need to teach them to be honest, not to pilfer from the storeroom or the cash register. They need to know that character is what you do when no one is looking. To us these seem obvious standards of employee conduct, but to someone who has never had a working adult as a role model, it is new territory.

Third, educate them about the "job of getting a job." Help them develop their sense of purpose with daily lists of things to do to find a job. Provide resources such as computers for writing résumés and cover letters. There are many ways that churches and community groups can assist former inmates to obtain a good job. Survey what job sources are currently available in your community, and refer them to employment organizations, where available, particularly those with experience serving homeless populations.

Create access to employers who might hire them. Teach them where to go to learn about job openings and ways to respond to job openings. Role-play with them concerning how to tell an employer about their criminal background and their desire to restructure their lives. Help them overcome the procrastination, fear of rejection, and discouragement that can sabotage any job search process.

Once they get a job, visit ex-inmates when they are at work. Role-play standards of behavior at work. Become acquainted with the boss and make your organization available if problems arise. Work on problem solving for the new employees. Provide "coaching" on what they are doing well at work as well as on areas for improvement. Work with them to develop goals concerning how long a period of employment will last. They may go through several employers before they find the right match. Be patient, help them think through tough challenges at their job, and keep encouraging them.

Resources for this chapter can be found beginning on page 94.

CHAPTER 6

Access to Health Care

For many prisoners their incarceration is their first regular access to medical care. That is the good news. However, the quality of the care they receive is minimal and inconsistent. Serious medical conditions are often overlooked or left untreated until they become life threatening (and even then, care is often too little and too late). During my incarceration, the physician's assistants administered Motrin® for virtually every condition.

When inmates develop a dental problem that is any more serious than a cavity, they are given a choice between having the tooth pulled and letting it rot. That is why you see so many inmates with teeth missing. While that saves taxpayers money, it certainly doesn't make the offenders more likely to get employment when they return from prison.

While imprisoned, they are exposed to many communicable diseases. The rates of hepatitis C, tuberculosis, HIV, and staph infections among prison inmates are skyrocketing. Many of these cases go undiagnosed in prison and come to light only in post-release medical examinations. Unfortunately, many prisoners are released with no provision for continuing their medication and treatment. If their treatment is interrupted, they risk developing drug-resistant viral strains that can spread within the community. It is very important that they be seen by medical personnel as soon as possible after their release.

Even worse are the problems faced by inmates with mental illness. There are three times as many men and women with mental illness in U.S. prisons as in mental hospitals. The largest forensic mental health facility in the world is the Los Angeles County Jail! This is a horrible situation. It was not caused by the prison system, but rather by the well-meaning effort to de-institutionalize the mentally ill. When the state mental hospitals were emptied, however, there were not sufficient resources allocated to treat the patients in community facilities. Without access to community treatment, the mentally ill simply roam the streets until the police respond to their erratic behavior by arresting them.

By default, prisons have become the dumping ground for the mentally ill. Prisons are dangerous and damaging places for the mentally ill, who are often victimized and exploited by other prisoners. In response to intimidation, some mentally ill prisoners withdraw into their cells, where the isolation makes their symptoms worse. Others strike back and are sent to "the hole," where they are less likely to receive psychiatric care. The symptoms of mental illness—such as being noisy, refusing orders, mutilating themselves, or attempting suicide—often bewilder prison officials, who take the easiest but most damaging route, either knocking them out with strong antipsychotic drugs and warehousing them in their cells or placing them in isolation, which can push them over the edge into acute psychosis.

Because mentally ill prisoners are commonly undiagnosed and/or untreated, community groups who serve them after release face the challenge of sorting out their confusing behaviors and obtaining accurate diagnoses and treatment. Homeless, mentally ill ex-offenders are sometimes turned away from supportive housing when their needs are considered too severe. Unfortunately, these men and women end up in single-room occupancy housing and emergency shelters, without any structure or support for their transition.

Follow-up to community-based care upon reentry is also usually superficial. Parole agencies are generally ill equipped to identify and address the mental-health needs of released prisoners. A national survey of parole administrators found that less than a quarter of the respondents indicated that they provide special programs for parolees with mental illness.

Whether inmates are ill with medical problems or mental illness, many prisons give them only a few days' supply of their medication upon release. Most offenders do not have medical insurance, and current law won't allow them to apply for Medicare until *after* they are released. This means that there is almost always a gap, ranging from days to months, between release and approval for health benefits. This gap can be a major obstacle to continuity of the care received in prison. During this time, the community is at risk. It is in the public interest that returning inmates get medical and mental-health treatment as soon as possible.

There are several ways you and your congregation can help inmates get the medical and mental-health care they need:

Provide individual assistance. Many ex-offenders are intimidated by the frustrations of paperwork, abrupt personnel, long waits, etc., that confront all of us in medical offices. Their experience in prison may not make them adept at handling these difficulties politely. You can provide a valuable service as their advocate and mediator if they are stymied by the bureaucracy.

- Assist the ex-offenders in filling out paperwork for Medicare benefits. Help them schedule appointments, and remind them of the importance of keeping them.

- Discuss how they intend to get to the appointment. You can assist them with understanding bus routes and schedules.
- Offer to go to their appointments with them. Be sensitive to their desire for privacy, but realize that they may be grateful to have a friend accompany them.
- If you are mentoring inmates still in prison, you can get some of the planning and paperwork done before their release.

Coordinate with local agencies. Because of the significant risks to public health and safety, most local public health agencies and police departments are eager to assist returning prisoners in getting the medical and mental-health treatment they need.

- Contact your local public health agencies to coordinate medical and mental-health services in the community so that ex-prisoners are assessed and treated as soon as possible.

- Work with local housing agencies to find structured and supportive housing for those ex-offenders with special medical needs or mental illness. Help them understand how life behind bars affects prisoners with these problems. Work with them to help the ex-offenders increase their skill and capacity to respond to their diseases rather than simply ban them from the housing.

Advocate for reforms. You and your congregation can help change the governmental policies that place barriers between offenders and appropriate health care. You should urge your representatives to change these policies so that prior to prisoners' release, the prison medical team will:

- Test for communicable diseases.
- Complete paperwork for post-release medical coverage.
- Schedule the inmates' first appointment for appropriate medical care.
- Provide inmates with copies of their medical records.
- Give inmates a sufficient supply of medications to cover them until their scheduled appointment.

Resources for this chapter can be found beginning on page 101.

CHAPTER 7

Freedom from Addiction

"Releasing drug and alcohol addicts and abusers without treatment or training is tantamount to visiting criminals on society."

—Joseph Califano, Jr.,
former Secretary of Health, Education and Welfare,
President of Center for Alcohol and Substance
Abuse (CASA)

There is no way to discuss the topic of returning prisoners without dealing with addiction to drugs and alcohol. According to the Center for Alcohol and Substance Abuse (CASA) at Columbia University, 80 percent of inmates were involved with drugs or alcohol before entering prison. They violated drug or alcohol laws, were high at the time of their offense, stole property to buy drugs, had histories of drug and alcohol abuse or addiction, or shared some mix of these characteristics.

The circle of pain that emanates from drug use is wide indeed. Children of drug-using inmates are three times more likely to be abused than are children of drug-free parents. They are also at high risk of addiction and criminal activity themselves. James Shields, an ex-offender and recovered addict who works as a staff leader of Delaware's Key program, notes that today's participants are younger and angrier than when he went through the program 13 years ago. "These are the sons and nephews we left on their own to raise themselves," he says. Without treatment, the iniquities of the fathers may indeed pass down to following generations (Exodus 34:7).

It seems logical that with the overwhelming problems associated with drug abuse, drug treatment would be a high priority inside prison. It isn't. In-prison treatment is not available to most of the inmates who need it. Nationally, only 10 percent of state prisoners in 1997 reported receiving formal substance abuse treatment, down from 25 percent in 1991. Joseph Califano, former secretary of Health, Education and Welfare and currently president of CASA, said, "Releasing drug and alcohol addicts and abusers without treatment or training is tantamount to visiting criminals on society."

The numbers bear him out. Only 41 percent of first-time offenders have a history of regular drug use. However, the figure rises to 81 percent of those with five or more convictions. The failure to deal with these inmates' addictions puts all of us at risk. The National Institute of Justice reports that 60 to 75 percent of untreated prisoners with histories of heroin or cocaine abuse return to using drugs within three months of their release from prison and resume their criminal activity.

An ex-offender's relapse into drug use is almost always accompanied with the loss of their job, eviction from his or her residence, family crisis, and rearrest. Social workers say that substance abuse is the single most important issue for ex-prisoners to work on if they are to avoid going back to prison.

Califano maintains that many of these addicts "would be law-abiding, working, taxpaying citizens and responsible parents, if they lived sober lives." The question is, can they be helped to lead sober lives? The answer is clearly "Yes."

- The Texas Criminal Justice Policy Council found that

only 7 percent of those who completed the state's substance-abuse program recidivated within two years, compared with a recidivism rate of 25 to 31 percent for those who failed to complete the treatment program. They found that the state of Texas saved $29.9 million as a result of diverting prison- or jail-bound offenders into a state drug program.

- A Vera Institute of Justice study of La Bodega de La Familia participants found that regular cocaine use dropped from 42 percent to 10 percent after six months. The comparison group showed a much smaller decrease, from 27 percent to 21 percent. More important, though, the study found that this drop in drug use appeared to stem not from additional time in drug treatment, but rather from a combination of pressure and encouragement from family members and focused support for family members.

- A California study concluded that effective treatment for drug offenders can generate a "seven-to-one return on investment"—primarily through a reduction in repeat criminal activity, a decrease in hospitalizations, and an increase in employment of reformed drug users.

- The Volunteers of America found that criminal behavior was substantially reduced after women participants completed their drug-treatment program. During the year before treatment, the women committed crimes on about half the days that they were at risk. During the year after treatment, their criminal activity dropped by more than half, from 50 percent of their days involved in crime to only 22 percent of their days. That amounts to 11,500 fewer "crime-days," and much safer communities.

- The Oregon Recovery Consortium found that in the first year after drug treatment, arrests dropped by 37 percent.

- The Delaware Life Skills Program reported that two years after release, female participants had a 15-percent recidivism rate versus a 50-percent rate for the comparison group.

Just as it is clear that addicts can become free of their addictions, the evidence is also clear that the Church can play a critical role in transforming their lives. In "*So Help Me God: Substance Abuse, Religion and Spirituality,*" the first study of the impact of religion on treatment of substance abuse, CASA President Joseph Califano, Jr., declared: "If ever the sum were greater than the parts, it is in combining the power of God, religion and spirituality with the power of science and professional medicine to prevent and treat substance abuse and addiction."

However, Califano added, "too often, clergy and physicians, religion and science are like ships passing in the night. When we separate the worlds of medicine and spirituality, we deny effective help to a host of individuals with substance abuse problems."

The study found that among mental-health professionals who treat substance abusers, more than half of those surveyed said they don't believe in God, and many would not recommend that their patients seek out a member of the clergy for help.

The Church for its part has largely left the field to these secularists. CASA found that while 94 percent of the pastors, priests, and rabbis surveyed consider drug abuse an important issue in their congregations, only 36 percent preach a sermon on the issue even once a year, and a mere 12.5 percent of these clergy had received any training in how to address it. What a sad commentary on the Church. It is "absent without leave" from one of the fiercest battles for the souls of our young people.

Some of the ways the Church can help returning offenders stay clean and sober are;

Help place ex-offenders in a drug-treatment program. Helping to smooth the transition from prison to home by connecting the returning offender to community-based treatment—immediately upon release or as soon thereafter as possible—could reduce the resumption of drug use and the likelihood of re-incarceration. Even better, start a Christ-centered recovery program in your church.

Provide positive relationships and activities. Coming back to the old neighborhood and seeing familiar places and former friends associated with drugs is particularly likely to increase cravings for drugs and alcohol. Ex-prisoners in recovery from addiction are therefore more likely to thrive, and stay clean and sober, with new friends and activities.

Deal with the ex-offender's family as a whole. The ex-offender's spouse, children, parents, and siblings have all been painfully wounded by addiction and imprisonment. They all have a stake in, and should be part of, the offender's recovery. La Bodega de la Familia works with the entire family to improve the health and functioning of family members and promote support for the user. Each person participates in the program with at least one family member, who attends weekly case management sessions.

Help with the necessities of life. The lack of a place to live, no job, no family or social supports all increase the risk of backsliding into drug use and crime. La Bodega helps with all the needs of the families. They believe that if family members' needs are met, they are better able to support the drug user in treatment and respond constructively to any relapses. Providing ongoing access to counseling and health care, practical assistance, and a good support network— including a church family—not only benefits the ex-prisoners but also, as a result, fosters public safety.

Encourage your pastor to get involved. Ask him or her to receive training on how to recognize signs of substance abuse and alcoholism and how to deal with them. Clergy should incorporate prevention and recovery messages into their ministry and become familiar with treatment services in their communities.

Educate medical professionals about the importance of faith in recovery. Tell them about CASA's research and website, and the other resources listed in the Resources section. Work with them to make faith a part of their treatment. Encourage them to take advantage of spiritual and religious resources available in your local community.

God offers hope to all His creatures, even junkies. "A bruised reed he will not break, and a smoldering wick he will not snuff out" (Isaiah 42:3). God doesn't write off drug abusers, and neither can we.

Resources for this chapter can be found beginning on page 108.

CHAPTER 8

Repairing the Harm Done by Crime

Crime harms people, and it should be our goal to repair that damage. Victims of crime are often ignored in our justice system. Most offenders are not held accountable to repay their victims. That's because our criminal justice system defines crime as an offense against the state, not against the victim. You can see this in the way criminal cases are titled: State v. Defendant. Crime is defined as "law breaking" rather than "victim harming," and the purpose of the criminal justice system is to maintain order by punishing the offenders for breaking the law and trying to ensure that they do not break the law again. Unfortunately, this leaves the victim out in the cold.

The Church should fill this void left for victims in our system. In the parable of the Good Samaritan (Luke 10:30-37), Jesus made it clear that crime victims are our neighbors; that it is our responsibility to bind their wounds and care for them until they are healed. Victims may sustain physical injury, monetary loss, and emotional suffering. The crime may disrupt their lives temporarily—or for as long as they live. To be victimized is to feel powerless, and victims often need help regaining an appropriate sense of control over their lives. Victims also need to be vindicated—

declared "not guilty" of being victimized.

The Church can provide practical, emotional, and spiritual assistance to victims of crime. Some of the ways you can help victims are:

- Provide immediate relief, such as food, lodging, house cleaning, medical care, and crime-scene cleanup.
- Accompany them to court; let them know you are there to support them.
- Keep them informed of the status of their case.
- Drive them to doctors' appointments.
- Help them complete applications for reimbursement for losses from victim restitution funds.
- Make their home more secure.
- Spend time with them. Companionship is important.
- Listen to them and make sure they realize that they are not at fault and did not deserve what happened to them.
- Pray with them.
- Find out how they can be informed of any parole hearing on their case.

It is important that you do *not* tell them that they must forgive the offender. At the appropriate time, the Holy Spirit will work in their hearts. It is not up to us to push them toward forgiveness.

However, victims often want to meet with their offenders and are sometimes even moved to forgive them. There are several excellent programs that prepare victims and offenders for such a meeting. These Victim-Offender programs are called by various names: reconciliation, mediation, or dialogue. Victims who choose to participate are given the opportunity to express their true feelings about what occurred, ask questions of the offender, and suggest ways that the offender can begin to make things right. According to assessments of several programs in the Midwest, victims' goals were to recover some losses, help the offenders stay out of trouble, and have a real part in the criminal justice process. This is something to be encouraged, but not rushed into.

If the victim wishes to meet with the offender, careful groundwork needs to be laid, lest an insincere or unapologetic offender cause further damage to the victim. However, when the victim and offender are ready, the opportunity for healing is miraculous. One of the most moving stories is that of Arna Washington and Ron Flowers. Mrs. Washington's daughter, Dee Dee, was waiting for her boyfriend, who unbeknownst to her was buying drugs. Her boyfriend and the dealer got into a struggle, and as the dealer, Ron Flowers, ran out of the building, he pulled a gun, and shot Dee Dee Washington as she sat in the car. Dee Dee died, and Ron Flowers went to prison for murder.

For 14 years, Ron denied murdering Dee Dee. Then he was admitted to the InnerChange Freedom Initiative (IFI), the prison program operated by Prison Fellowship in Texas. An important part of the IFI curriculum is Sycamore Tree, a program in which victims of crime tell the inmates the pain caused by their crime. While these aren't the actual victims of the inmates' crimes, for many of the inmates it is the first time they have to confront the real pain they have caused. By hearing these painful stories, most are brought to the point of remorse. The inmates are encouraged to make things right with their actual victim, and when their victim is willing, to seek their forgiveness.

During one of these Sycamore Tree sessions, Ron admitted that he did, in fact, murder Dee Dee Washington, and prayed that his victim's family would forgive him. He wrote a letter to Mrs. Washington expressing his deep remorse.

For her part, Mrs. Washington had written angry letters to the parole board every year of Ron's sentence, urging them to deny him parole. However, the same week that Ron confessed, Mrs. Washington had felt an overwhelming conviction that she should meet with the man who had killed her daughter. As she said later, she had no intention of forgiving him. Instead, she wanted to tell him how much pain he had caused her. She contacted her pastor and requested to meet with him.

Her pastor tracked Ron down at IFI. After Prison Fellowship staff met with Mrs. Washington and Ron Flowers separately several times to prepare them for the meeting, Mrs. Washington; her pastor, Homer Williams; IFI Director Jack Cowley; and Ron Flowers got together. She had the chance to ask the questions that virtually every victim wants to ask: "Why did you do it?" "Was my daughter involved in some way?" "How did it happen?" Ron filled her in on the details and reassured her that her daughter had no idea that a drug deal was taking place. As Ron told her the story of the day he killed Dee Dee, Mrs. Washington took his hands in hers and said, "I forgive you."

I was in Houston for Ron's graduation from IFI. As Ron crossed the stage to receive his diploma, a tall, elegant woman rose from her seat and walked up to meet him. Mrs. Washington embraced Ron, the man who had murdered her daughter, and told all of us in the audience, "This young man is my adopted son."

After his release, Mrs. Washington helped Ron adjust to the community, invited him to sit with her in her pew at church, had him over for dinner at her home, and even stood by him for his marriage. This beautiful ending to a very sad story could only happen through God's grace. Only He can bring about such reconciliation and healing.

Most inmates do not have the opportunity to participate in a program such as IFI, and therefore have not acknowledged the harm they have done to their victims, nor have they taken any steps to make things right with them. Whether or not the court has required restitution for the crime, morally the offenders should take steps, as appropriate, to repair the harm they have done. In Luke 19:8-9: "Zacchaeus [the corrupt tax collector] stood up and said to Jesus, 'Look, Lord . . . if I have cheated anybody out of anything, I will pay back four times the amount.' Jesus said to him, 'Today salvation has come to this house.'"

This is the soul of Restorative Justice: In the face of devastation brought by crime, God calls His people to restore, to rebuild, and to facilitate right relationships. You and your congregation can be agents of this healing grace by participating in one of the victim/offender ministries listed in the Resources section of this book.

There is another group of crime victims who need very special attention as offenders move from prison to their communities: their families.

More than 1.5 million children have a parent in prison. Maintaining strong family ties during imprisonment has a positive impact on both returning prisoners and their children. Several studies have shown that continued contact with family members during and following incarceration reduces recidivism and helps the offender reintegrate into the community.

Yet, the prison experience severely tests family connections. Imprisonment typically prevents the prisoner from providing meaningful financial and emotional support. Family members left behind may feel abandoned and resentful of the prisoner and the incarceration. Maintaining connections and bonds with family members during the prison term through visits, phone calls, and letters is challenging. The average prisoner is incarcerated more than 100 miles from home, so arranging visits can present many obstacles for the family.

In addition, prison visits can be unpleasant experiences for family members who are frequently treated like criminals themselves. My children had never seen their mother disrespected until a prison officer at the visitors desk screamed at her when she set our 10-month-old son down on the counter to get her license out of her purse. He spat at Gail, "You can't start a second line. Get back in line." She felt humiliated and the children were stunned.

Because visits are infrequent at best, phone calls are a lifeline between inmates and their families. Yet, prison phone calls are prohibitively expensive. In some institutions, weekly 30-minute telephone calls can total $125 per month. Most prisons prohibit prisoners' families from taking advantage of lower-cost collect call plans.

Since in-person visits and phone calls are few and far between, many programs have been developed to retain the bonds of family during the very difficult time of incarceration and transition back to the community. Some help parents record tapes of books, which are then sent home to their children so that they can hear their parents reading them a bedtime story. The Salvation Army videotaped a message from me to my wife and children, which became a treasured link between us while I was away.

One program that is particularly meaningful to my family is Prison Fellowship's Angel Tree®. Volunteers from local churches deliver Christmas presents to prisoners' children in the name of their incarcerated parent. They pray with the family, share the Gospel, and invite them to their church. As my first Christmas in prison approached, I was anxious about how I would show my children that I still loved them. I knew that Christmas is about far more than presents, but in our culture they are important ways of showing our love. I was stuck in prison camp, and powerless to make or buy anything for my children. Then we found some Angel Tree applications in the prison chapel, and I filled one out. This was answered prayer!

A few days before Christmas, a family from the local Baptist Church came by our house to give each of our children beautiful clothes and toys. "This is from your dad," they told my excited children. Then they told them about the birth of Christ and the Good News of what He had done for us all. My children still talk to me about those presents I "gave" them. As my wife, Gail, closed the door after the nice family left, Courtney, our eldest daughter, turned to her and said, "I knew Daddy would remember."

She had never mentioned to Gail that she was worried I *wouldn't* remember them at Christmas; it was obvious that her little heart had been troubled by the possibility. I was powerless to do anything about it, but those wonderful people from the local church were the arms of the body of Christ, reaching out in love to help keep the bonds of my family together.

Resources for this chapter can be found beginning on page 116.

CHAPTER 9

Restoring the Community

"We [should] no longer view offenders as tax consuming recipients of correctional services, but rather as a legion of citizens capable of doing something significant to build better and safer communities."

—Dr. Gordon Bazemore,
Director of the Community Justice Institute
Florida Atlantic University

Crime injures more than the direct victims and the families of offenders; it also disrupts the peace of the community, sowing fear and distrust. Offenders have a responsibility to make amends for the harm they have done to the community as well as to their victims. The Church can encourage offender repentance and help offenders earn their way back into the "good graces" of the community by doing something of value for their neighborhood.

Dennis Maloney, the former director of Community Justice in Deschutes County, Oregon, encourages offenders to pursue this "Earned Redemption" through community service projects that benefit the community by helping the disadvantaged, promoting economic development, or improving the general quality of life. Neighborhood groups and crime victims often have excellent suggestions for the work projects for the offenders.

In return for their work on these projects, offenders:

- Become involved in meaningful community-building activities.
- Learn marketable skills.
- Become productive, responsible members of the community.
- Learn about the effect of their behavior on the community and work to bring some form of reparation back to the community for their part in eroding the community's sense of peace.

People who share a strong sense of community are far less likely to violate the trust of others. It is in the public's best interest to increase offenders' sense of community. Imagine the transformation that would occur in our neighborhoods if the legions of ex-offenders were to work on community service projects, such as: building homes for poor families, working in shelters for the homeless, constructing neighborhood clinics, building and maintaining playgrounds and athletic fields, or serving meals in senior centers.

You and your church can organize community service projects for returning inmates. In considering which projects to undertake, Maloney suggests you ask:

- What services does the victim want or need?
- What important community projects are currently planned or underway that could benefit from offenders' contribution?
- What are the offenders good at, or what skills do they have to contribute to the community?
- What career interests do the offenders have, and how

can service be linked to those careers?

- What does the community need to become a more peaceful place?
- What behaviors or addictions, without necessary treatment, stand in the way of the offenders being able to contribute?
- How can service best complement that treatment and build relationships that reduce the likelihood of recidivism?
- What type of service can be performed to allow offenders to earn money to pay back their crime victim?

The work project should provide a tangible benefit to the community and be of such a public nature that the community sees the work performed by ex-offenders. Then the public will see them as the "nice people" who built the new playground, served meals at the senior center, or built the home for the low-income seniors down the block, rather than the "ex-cons" at the halfway house. This will encourage the community to accept these offenders who have "made amends" for the harm they have caused.

Offenders will take pride in the work they have accomplished, and their work will lay the foundation for building positive relationships in the community. Long after they have completed their sentence, the ex-offenders will be able to see the project they had a part in building for their community.

Here are examples of some of community service projects that have been performed by offenders in communities around the country:

- In Alabama, offenders insulated and repaired the home of an aged couple who had recently been robbed. For this couple the service project filled a physical need. But more, it helped them overcome the traumatization of victimization. As for the inmates, they were able to symbolically pay back the community they had harmed and earn a new element of self-respect.

- In inner-city Pittsburgh, young offenders in an intensive day treatment program solicit input from community organizations about service projects the organizations would like to see completed in the neighborhood. The offenders then work with community residents on projects that include home repair and gardening for the elderly, voter registration drives, painting homes and public buildings, and planting and cultivating community gardens.

- In South Florida, youthful offenders, sponsored by the Florida Department of Juvenile Justice and supervised by The 100 Black Men of Palm Beach County, Inc., plan and execute projects that provide shelter for the care and treatment of abused, abandoned, and HIV positive/AIDS-infected infants and children.

- In Cleveland, ex-offenders mentor young offenders in juvenile justice programs, and work with churches to provide shopping and support services for the home-bound elderly.

- In Dakota County, a Minneapolis suburb, local retailers and senior citizens whose businesses and homes have been damaged by burglary or vandalism call a crime repair "hotline" to request a work crew of probationers to repair the damage.

- In Deschutes County, Oregon, juvenile offender

work crews cut and deliver firewood to senior citizens. They also worked with a local contractor to build a homeless shelter.

- In several Montana cities, college students and other young adult "core members" in the Montana Conservation Corps supervise juvenile offenders on environmental restoration, trail building, and other community service projects. These students also serve as mentors to one or more of the young offenders.

When offenders have completed their sentence, worked to repair harm to their victims and the community, and curtailed their offensive behavior, there is one last piece of restoration to be accomplished: They should be afforded the opportunity to participate as members in good standing in the community.

When the judge brings the gavel down and sentences offenders to prison, it is a formal banishment that takes away their rights as citizens. After they have paid their debt to society, it is equally important that there be a point at which they are welcomed back as full members of the community. Many states have laws that permanently deprive convicted felons of their right to vote. That is wrong, and those laws should be changed. As Chuck Colson has said: "I believe all ex-cons should be given back their rights after a time if they show they are living a responsible life." We are "called to a ministry of reconciliation" (2 Corinthians 5:18). Certainly restoring citizenship to those who are living clean, productive lives should be part of that reconciliation.

This book has provided examples of the Church working with community institutions to repair the harm done by crime. This is Restorative Justice in action: Offenders are held responsible for their actions. Victims are restored financially and emotionally. The sense of community is restored by service to the community. Families are knit more closely together.

I am often asked what America's communities would look like if biblical principles of justice were implemented. Such a "vision statement" was written by God long ago in Isaiah 32:18: "My people will live in peaceful dwelling places, in secure homes, and in undisturbed places of rest." This is a glimpse of the peace, or *shalom*, a vision of what God intends our communities to be.

This is God's plan for us. You, your community, and your church have important roles to play in making your neighborhood peaceful, secure, and tranquil. One of the most important areas in which you can make a difference is in the lives of returning offenders.

Resources for this chapter can be found beginning on page 132.

Resources

The organizations listed in this Resources section of *When Prisoners Return* provide much-needed assistance to returning prisoners, and they are included so that churches and community groups might learn how others are serving ex-offenders. Prison Fellowship does not necessarily endorse these groups and programs. Also, there are most certainly other groups that are doing great work in this field. We have not intentionally left any out, and would appreciate learning about others that are involved in this important work.

Resources for Chapter 1: *"600,000 Offenders Returning Home"*

PRISON FELLOWSHIP PROGRAMS

Prison Fellowship: *"Aftercare: Developing a Church-Based Ministry for Ex-Prisoners"*
Prison Fellowship has produced excellent training materials to assist churches in planning and developing their own ministries to ex-prisoners returning to their communities. PF will help the church customize its services according to the resources of its congregation and the needs of the community. Find out how to contact the nearest local Prison Fellowship office by calling toll-free (877) 478-0100.
National Office
P.O. Box 1550
Merrifield, VA 22116-1550
Phone: (703) 478-0100
www.prisonfellowship.org

The InnerChange Freedom Initiative (IFI) is a partnership between the state Department of Corrections and Prison Fellowship that prepares inmates for their return to society with the goal of reducing recidivism—through a 24-hour-a-day, 7-day-a-week values-based program taught from a biblical perspective. The in-prison phase is followed by a post-release phase that includes church involvement and mentoring. All prisoner participants volunteer for the program. IFI programs are currently operating in Texas, Iowa, Minnesota, and Kansas.
P.O. Box 1550
Merrifield, VA 22116-1550
Phone: (703) 478-0100 x 3729
www.ifiprison.org

Justice Fellowship, the criminal justice reform arm of Prison Fellowship, has a website with many issue papers, legislative updates, and resources related to prisoner reentry. While at the website please subscribe to the *Justice eReport*, a weekly e-mail update on criminal justice issues, legislation, and resources.
P.O. Box 1550
Merrifield, VA 22116-1550
Phone: (800) 217-2743
www.justicefellowship.org

GENERAL RESOURCES

National Religious Affairs Association is an affiliate of the National Association of Blacks in Criminal Justice, which encourages cooperation between criminal justice professionals and the faith community.
P.O. Box 77075
Washington, DC 20013-7075
Phone: (703) 765-4459
Fax: (703) 765-9761
www.nabcj.org

The Office of Justice Programs *Reentry* website, www.ojp. usdoj.gov/reentry, has many excellent resources.

Reentry National Media Outreach Campaign is designed to support the work of community and faith-based organizations through offering media resources that will facilitate community discussion and decision making about solution-based reentry programs.
http://www.reentrymediaoutreach.org/index.html

Restorative Justice Ministry Network of North America is an excellent source for a variety of ministries to ex-offenders.
1232 Avenue J
Huntsville, TX 77340
Phone: (936) 291-2156
http://66.96.187.49/welcome.htm

Transition of Prisoners® works to encourage, train, and support local churches in building their capacity to more effectively minister to prisoners, ex-prisoners in transition, and their families.
P.O. Box 02938
Detroit, MI 48202
Phone: (313) 875-3883
www.topinc.net/index.htm

The Urban Institute has developed much useful information as part of their effort to strengthen community strategies for prisoners returning to society.
Urban Institute
2100 M Street, NW
Washington, DC 20037
Phone: (202) 833-7200
http://www.urban.org/template.cfm?Template=/TaggedCont
ent/ViewPublication.cfm&PublicationID=8700&NavMenuI
D=95

The Vera Institute of Justice website, www.vera.org, has several very helpful resources including the *Safe Return Initiative* and *Project Greenlight*.

PROGRAMS

Catholic Charities of the Archdiocese of New York
1011 First Avenue
New York, NY 10022
Phone: (212) 371-1000
www.ny-archdiocese.org

Champions for Life (formerly Bill Glass Ministries)
(Holds evangelistic "Weekend of Champions" events in prisons across the county)
P.O. Box 761101
Dallas, TX 75376-1101
Phone (972) 298-1101
www.lifechampions.org

Coalition of Prison Evangelists (COPE) (Provides resources and referrals for prison-related ministry)
P.O. Box 210252
Bedford, TX 76095
Phone: (888) 256-2673
www.copeministries.org

Crossroads Prison Ministries (Founded by Nick Barbetta, an ex-offender turned prison chaplain; helps ex-offenders reintegrate back into the community.)
P.O. Box 363
Bensalem, PA 19020
Phone: (215) 639-8145
Fax: (215) 639-8149
http://crossroadspm.gospelcom.net/ex-offenders.php

Episcopal Social Services
305 Seventh Avenue, Fourth Floor
New York, NY 10001-6008
Phone: (212) 675-1000
Fax: (212) 989-1132

Exodus Transitional Community (Provides support to people who are moving from incarceration to full reintegration into their communities.)
161 East 104th Street
New York, NY 10029
Phone: (917) 492-0990
Fax: (917) 492-8711
www.etcny.org
See also, Marks, Alexandra. "Ex-cons Help Ex-cons Ease into Life on Outside." *Christian Science Monitor*. May 7, 2001.

Going Home Initiative (North Carolina's transition and reentry plan for offenders released from prison. This is targeted at serious and violent adults with at least 90 days of community service.)
http://www.doc.state.nc.us/rap/goinghome.htm

Good News Jail and Prison Ministry (Places chaplains in prisons and jails around the U.S. to minister to inmates and prepare them for new life in the community)
2230 E. Parham Road
Richmond, VA 23228
Phone: (804) 553-4090
www.goodnewsjail.org

Harvest Ministry of Oklahoma (Helps ex-offenders reintegrate into society.)
P.O. Box 15376
Oklahoma City, OK 73155

Life Changing Ministries
5550 Baltimore National Pike
Cantonsville, MD 21228
Phone: (410) 747-8015
www.life-changing.org

Maryland Re-Entry Partnership Initiative (Collaboration between community-based and government organizations to provide services to inmates both pre-release and post-release.)
www.ci.baltimore.md.us/government/mocj/reentry.html

National Foundation for Consumer Credit (A nonprofit credit counseling organization that helps consumers manage debt, set up budgets, and contact creditors.)
Phone: (800) 388-2227
www.nfcc.org

Surviving the System (Helps ex-offenders reenter society through guidance, support, and education.)
P.O. Box 1860
Ridgeland, MS 39158
Phone: (601) 898-8331
http://www.survivingthesystem.com/reentry.htm

BOOKS, ARTICLES AND VIDEOS

MacDonald, Heather "How to Straighten Out Ex-Cons." *City Journal*, Spring 2003. http://www.city-journal.org/html/13_2_how_to_straighten.html

Petersilia, Joan. *When Prisoners Come Home*, Oxford University Press, 2003 http://www.oup.co.uk/isbn/0-19-516086-X Reviewed on Justice Fellowship's website: http://www.pfm.org/JusticeTemplate.cfm?Section=Justice_Home&template=/ContentManagement/ContentDisplay.cfm&ContentID=11785

Prison Fellowship. *Aftercare: Developing a Church-Based Ministry for Ex-Prisoners* (training). Contact your local Prison Fellowship office by calling (877) 478-0100 or visiting online at www.pfmonline.net/CCOM_ZipSearch.taf

"Reentry Partnership Initiative: Moving From *Prison Safety* to *Public Safety*." University of Maryland and Sponsored by the National Institute of Justice, 2000. http://www.bgr.umd.edu/pdf/RPI.collection.pdf

Sull, Errol C., and Catherine M. Skora. *Makin' It: A Parole and Probation Survival Guide*. Aardvark Publishing, 2000.

Taxman, Faye S. and Douglas Young "Offender's Views of Reentry: Implications for Processes, Programs and Services." U.S. Department of Justice. August 20, 2002. http://www.ncjrs.org/pdffiles1/nij/grants/196490.pdf

The Urban Institute has released a brief on the findings of its study of prisoner reentry, *Returning Home: Understanding the Challenges of Prisoner Reentry*. Significantly, of the factors that returning inmates found useful in the first months after release, "church/mosque" (6.9%) ranked third behind "family" (20%) and "substance abuse treatment" (11%) and above "having a job" (6.2%), "social services" (4.8%), etc. http://www.urban.org/UploadedPDF/310946_ BaltimorePrisoners.pdf

Wilkinson, Reginald, Ed.D., Director Ohio Department of Rehabilitation and Correction, (Paper prepared for Third National Forum on Restorative Justice, Sponsored by Justice Fellowship, Orlando, Florida, March 14-16, 2002.) *"Prisoners Reentering Society: Revisiting the Transition From Incarceration to the Community"* http://www.drc.state.oh.us/web/Articles/article98.htm

Resources for Chapter 2: *"A Changed Heart"*

PRISON FELLOWSHIP PROGRAMS

Prison Fellowship
Prison Fellowship has produced excellent Aftercare training materials to assist churches in planning and developing their own ministries to ex-prisoners returning to their communities. PF will help the church customize its services according to the resources of its congregation and the needs of the community. Find out how to contact the nearest local Prison Fellowship office by calling toll-free (877) 478-0100.
National Office
P.O. Box 1550
Merrifield, VA 22116-1550
Phone: (703) 478-0100
www.prisonfellowship.org

The InnerChange Freedom Initiative (IFI) is a partnership between the state Department of Corrections and Prison Fellowship that prepares inmates for their return to society with the goal of reducing recidivism—through a 24-hour-a-day, 7-day-a-week values-based program taught from a biblical perspective. The in-prison phase is followed by a post-release phase that includes church involvement and mentoring. All prisoner participants volunteer for the program. IFI programs are currently operating in Texas, Iowa, Minnesota, and Kansas.
P.O. Box 1550
Merrifield, VA 22116-1550
Phone: (703) 478-0100 x 3729
www.ifiprison.org

Justice Fellowship, the criminal justice reform arm of Prison Fellowship, has a website with many issue papers, legislative updates, and resources related to prisoner reentry. While at the website please subscribe to the *Justice eReport*, a weekly e-mail update on criminal justice issues, legislation, and resources.
P.O. Box 1550
Merrifield, VA 22116-1550
Phone: (800) 217-2743
www.justicefellowship.org

PROGRAMS

Alpha USA
74 Trinity Place, 10th Floor
New York, NY 10006
Phone: (888) 949-2574
Fax: (212) 406-7521
http://www.alphausa.org/contact/index.html

American Bible Society
1865 Broadway
New York, NY 10023
Phone: (212) 408-1200
www.americanbible.org

Association of Gospel Rescue Mission
1045 Swift Street
Kansas City, MO 64116-4127
Phone: (816) 471-8020
Fax: (816) 471-3718
www.agrm.org

Billy Graham Center
Wheaton College
Wheaton, IL
Phone: (630) 752-5157
Fax: (630) 752-5916
www.bgc.gospelcom.net

Campus Crusade for Christ International
100 Lake Hart Drive
Orlando, FL 32832
Phone: (407) 826-2000
www.ccci.org

Catholic Charities of the Archdiocese of New York
1011 First Avenue
New York, NY 10022
Phone: (212) 371-1000
www.ny-archdiocese.org

Community Bible Study
1765 Business Center Drive, Suite 200
Reston, VA 20190-5327
www.communitybiblestudy.org

Crossroad Bible Institute
P.O. Box 900
Grand Rapids, MI 49509-0900
Phone: (800) 668-2450
Fax: (616) 530-1302
www.crossroadbible.com

Faith Community Partnership
633 Indiana Ave., NW
Washington, DC 20004
Phone: 2020-220-5306
www.csosa.gov
See also "Starting Out, Starting Over, Staying Out: A Guide for District of Columbia Ex-Offenders: Housing, Food, Employment, and Other Resources."
http://www.csosa.gov/reentry/dc-cure.pdf

First Baptist Church Huntsville
1229 Avenue J
Huntsville, TX 77340
Phone: (936) 291-3441
Fax: (936) 291-1174
http://www.fbchuntsville.org/Restorative_Justice.htm

Great Dads
P.O. Box 7527
Fairfax Station, VA 22039
Phone: (888) 478-3237
www.greatdads.org

Intercessors for America
www.ifa-usapray.org

International Bible Society
1820 Jet Stream Drive
Colorado Springs, CO 80921
Phone: (719) 488-9200
www.ibs.org

Koinonia House® National Ministries
P.O. Box 1415
Wheaton, IL 60189-1415
Phone: (630) 221-9930
Fax: (630) 221-9932
http://www.koinoniahouse.org/Interface/Public/aboutus.asp

Lott Carey Foreign Mission Convention
300 I Street, NE, Suite 104
Washington, DC 20002-4389
Phone: (202) 543-3200
Fax: (202)543-6300
www.lottcarey.org

Mission America Coalition
P.O. Box 13930
Palm Desert, CA 92255
Phone: (760) 200-2707
Fax: (760) 200-8837
www.missionamerica.org

Moody Bible Institute
820 North LaSalle Blvd.
Chicago, IL 60610
Phone: (312) 329-4000
www.moody.edu

Morning Start Ministry
P.O. Box 571
Iowa City, IA 52244
www.morningstarministry.com

The Navigators
3820 N. 30th Street
Colorado Springs, CO 80934
Phone: (719) 598-1212
Fax: (719) 260-0479
www.home.navigators.org

North American Mission Board, SBC
4200 North Point Parkway
Alpharetta, GA 30022-4176
Phone: (770) 410-6000
Fax: (770) 410-6018
www.namb.net

Pittsburgh Leadership Foundation
100 Ross Street, 4th Floor
Pittsburgh, PA 15219
Phone: (412) 281-3752
Fax: (412) 281-2312
www.plf.org

Promise Keepers
P.O. Box 103001
Denver, CO 80250-3001
Phone: (800) 888-7595
www.promisekeepers.org

Ramah International
1776 Hudson Street
Englewood, FL 34223
Phone: (941) 473-2188
Fax: (941) 473-2248
www.ramahinternational.org

Salvation Army
Phone: (703) 684-5500
www.salvationarmyusa.org

Transition of Prisoners
P.O. Box 02938
Detroit, MI 48202
Phone: (313) 875-3883
www.topinc.net/index.htm

Walk Thru the Bible
http://www.christianity.com/walkthruthebible

Youth Direct Ministries
P.O. Box 380520
Duncanville, TX 75138-0520
Phone: (972) 572-8336
Fax: (972) 572-8335
www.youthdirect.org

ARTICLES, BOOKS, AND VIDEOS
Hidalgo, Ellie. "Christian Values Can Guide Justice Polices." Tidings Online, March 21, 2003.
http://the-tidings.com/2003/0321/massingale.htm

Thorburn, Stan. "The Ministry of Reconciliation." St. George's Anglican Church, 7 December 2003. http://www.restorativejustice.org/rj3/chapel/Reconciliationsermon.pdf

Van Ness, Daniel. "Shalom" Restorative Justice.org http://www.restorativejustice.org/rj3/chapel/Shalom.html

Van Ness, Daniel W., and Karen Heetderks Strong. *Restoring Justice*, second edition. Cincinnati, OH: Anderson Pub., 2002

Zehr, Howard. "A Justice that Restores." *Christianity Today* (April 2004). http://www.christianitytoday.com/ct/2004/004/33.81.html

Resources for Chapter 3: *"A Welcoming Church and Loving Mentors"*

PRISON FELLOWSHIP PROGRAMS

Prison Fellowship
Prison Fellowship has produced excellent Aftercare and Mentoring training materials to assist churches in planning and developing their own ministries to ex-prisoners returning to their communities. PF will help the church customize its services according to the resources of its congregation and the needs of the community. Find out how to contact the nearest local Prison Fellowship office by calling toll-free (877) 478-0100.
National Office
P.O. Box 1550
Merrifield, VA 22116-1550
Phone: (703) 478-0100
www.prisonfellowship.org

The InnerChange Freedom Initiative (IFI) is a partnership between the state Department of Corrections and Prison Fellowship that prepares inmates for their return to society with the goal of reducing recidivism—through a 24-hour-a-day, 7-day-a-week values-based program taught from a biblical perspective. The in-prison phase is followed by a post-release phase that includes church involvement and mentoring. All prisoner participants volunteer for the program. IFI programs are currently operating in Texas, Iowa, Minnesota, and Kansas.
P.O. Box 1550
Merrifield, VA 22116-1550
Phone: (703) 478-0100 x 3729
www.ifiprison.org

Justice Fellowship, the criminal justice reform arm of Prison Fellowship, has a website with many issue papers, legislative updates, and resources related to prisoner reentry. While at the website please subscribe to the *Justice eReport*, a weekly e-mail update on criminal justice issues, legislation, and resources.
P.O. Box 1550
Merrifield, VA 22116-1550
Phone: (800) 217-2743
www.justicefellowship.org

PROGRAMS

Christian Mission Center, Inc. (An Alabama ministry that provides many services to the needy. Their website lists these services and a Christian "Twelve Step" program for addicts.)
www.christianmissioncentersinc.com

Conquest Offender Reintegration Ministries
P.O. Box 73873
Washington, DC 20056-3873
Phone: (202) 723-2015
http://www.conquesthouse.org/reintegration.html

Faith Community Partnership (Mentors serve as links to faith-based institution and help ex-offenders make the transition back into their community.)
633 Indiana Ave., NW
Washington, DC 20004
Phone: (202) 220-5306
www.csosa.gov
See also *Starting Out, Starting Over, Staying Out: A Guide for District of Columbia Ex-Offenders: Housing, Food, Employment, and Other Resources.*
http://www.csosa.gov/reentry/dc-cure.pdf

First Baptist Church Huntsville ("Welcome Back Program" helps families and ex-offenders at the time of release and helps them connect to the local faith community.)
1229 Avenue J
Huntsville, TX 77340
Phone: (936) 291-3441
Fax: (936) 291-1174
http://www.fbchuntsville.org/Restorative_Justice.htm

Koinonia House® **National Ministries** (Helps ex-prisoners make the transition back into communities and connects them to local churches.)
P.O. Box 1415
Wheaton, IL 60189-1415
Phone: (630) 221-9930
Fax: (630) 221-9932
http://www.koinoniahouse.org/Interface/Public/aboutus.asp

The Milwaukee Outreach Center (Unites churches and ministries to reach out to those in need of physical and spiritual help.)
724 S. Layton Blvd.
Milwaukee, WI 53215
Phone: (414) 385-2233
www.tmoc.org

National Baptist Convention USA, Prison Ministry and Criminal Justice Commission
2585 Van Buren Street
Gary, IN 46407
Phone: (219) 886-2541
Fax: (219) 886-9288
www.nationalbaptist.com

Prodigal Ministries (Aids ex-offenders through mentorship, Christian counseling, support groups, and employment assistance.)
1113 South Fourth Street
Louisville, KY 40203
Phone: (502) 775-0026

Rogers House (Helps with prisoner re-integration, mentoring, and assistance with housing and employment.)
934 Culver Road
Rochester, NY 14609
Phone: (716) 482-2694

St. Leonard's Ministries
2100 West Warren Blvd.
Chicago, IL 60612
Phone: (312) 738-1414
Fax: (312) 738-1417
www.kuc.org/agency/grace.htm

Ten Point Leadership Foundation (Mobilizes churches to combat urban violence in Boston.)
360 Huntington Avenue, Suite 140SC-401
Boston, MA 02115
Phone: (617) 373-7273
Fax: (617) 373-7575
vwillingham@ntlf.org
www.ntlf.org

Transition of Prisoners (Helps ex-offenders reintegrate into community by using faith institutions, mentoring, group interaction, and social service agencies.)
P.O. Box 02938
Detroit, MI 48202
Phone: (313) 875-3883
www.topinc.net/index.htm

US Dream Academy (Mentors and educates children of prisoners in technology and other academic subjects.)
10400 Little Patuxent Parkway, Suite 300
Columbia, MD 21044
Phone: (800) 873-7326
http://www.usdreamacademy.org/2002/main.asp

ARTICLES, BOOKS, AND VIDEOS ON CHURCH REENTRY PROGRAMS

"Empowering New Partnerships in Your Community: Faith-Based and Community Initiatives in the Workforce System."
http://www.in.gov/fssa/fathers/pdf/empoweringfinal.pdf

U.S. Department of Labor Center for Faith-Based and Community Initiatives
200 Constitution Avenue, NW
Washington, DC 20210
Phone: (202) 693-6150
www.dol.gov/cfbci

Jones, Louis. *Equipping Your Church to Minister to Ex-Offenders*. Conquest Offender Reintegration Ministries, 2000.
http://www.conquesthouse.org/equipping.htm

McRoberts, Omar M. "Religion, Reform, Community: Examining the Idea of Church-based Prisoner Reentry." Urban Institute. March 20, 2002.
http://www.urban.org/Template.cfm?NavMenuID=24&template=/TaggedContent/ViewPublication.cfm&PublicationID=8440

"One Church One Inmate Program Growing in Georgia," *The Georgia Bulletin*, 15 June 2000. http://www.georgiabulletin.org/local/2000/06/15/h

RESOURCES ON MENTORING

National Mentoring Center (Provides training and technical assistance to mentoring programs [juvenile] though a variety of services.)
Northwest Regional Educational Laboratory
101 SW Main Street, Suite 500
Portland, OR 97204
Phone: (503) 275-0135
Fax: (503) 275-0444
http://www.nwrel.org/mentoring/topic_faith.html

National Mentoring Partnership (Resources and information on how to mentor youth.)
http://www.mentoring.org

Public Private Ventures (Youth mentoring programs)
Amachi Mentoring Program
2000 Market Street, Suite 600
Philadelphia, PA 19103
Phone: (215) 557-4427
Fax: (215) 557-2270
http://www.ppv.org/ppv/publications/publications.asp

ARTICLES, BOOKS, AND VIDEOS ON MENTORING

Christian Mentoring of Former Prisoners. "Are You Called of God to Minister to Ex-Offenders?"
http://www.conquesthouse.org/mentoring.pdf

CSOSA/Faith Community Partnerships. Court Services and Offender Supervision Agency Faith-Based Mentoring Initiative.
http://www.csosa.gov/reentry/mentor_info.pdf
Most states have this program. See East of the River Clergy-Police-Community Partnership, Inc.
http://www.charityadvantage.com/ercpcp/MentorshipProgram.asp

National Mentoring Partnership Toolkit for Mentors
www.mentoring.org/training/TMT/index.adp
Office of Juvenile Justice and Delinquency Prevention (OJJDP) Juvenile Mentoring Program, "Coaching a Kid in the Game of Life . . . Be a Mentor."
http://ojjdp.ncjrs.org/mentoring/index.html

Resources for Chapter 4: *"A Safe Place to Live"*

PRISON FELLOWSHIP PROGRAMS

Prison Fellowship
Prison Fellowship has produced excellent Aftercare and Mentoring training materials to assist churches in planning and developing their own ministries to ex-prisoners returning to their communities. PF will help the church customize its services according to the resources of its congregation and the needs of the community. Find out how to contact the nearest local Prison Fellowship office by calling toll-free (877) 478-0100.
National Office
P.O. Box 1550
Merrifield, VA 22116-1550
Phone: (703) 478-0100
www.prisonfellowship.org

The InnerChange Freedom Initiative (IFI) is a partnership between the state Department of Corrections and Prison Fellowship that prepares inmates for their return to society with the goal of reducing recidivism—through a 24-hour-a-day, 7-day-a-week values-based program taught from a biblical perspective. The in-prison phase is followed by a post-release phase that includes church involvement and mentoring. All prisoner participants volunteer for the program. IFI programs are currently operating in Texas, Iowa, Minnesota, and Kansas.
P.O. Box 1550
Merrifield, VA 22116-1550
Phone: (703) 478-0100 x 3729
www.ifiprison.org

Justice Fellowship, the criminal justice reform arm of Prison Fellowship, has a website with many issue papers, legislative updates, and resources related to prisoner reentry. While at the website please subscribe to the *Justice eReport*, a weekly e-mail update on criminal justice issues, legislation, and resources.
P.O. Box 1550
Merrifield, VA 22116-1550
Phone: (800) 217-2743
www.justicefellowship.org

PROGRAMS

AIDS Housing of Washington—"From Locked Up to Locked Out"
AIDS Housing of Washington
2014 East Madison, Suite 200
Seattle, WA 98122
Phone: (206) 322-9444
Fax: (206) 322-9298
http://www.aidshousing.org/usr_doc/from_locked_up_to_lo
cked_out.pdf

Association of Gospel Rescue Mission (Provides emergency food and shelter, youth and family services, rehabilitation programs for the addicted, education and job training programs, and assistance to the elderly poor and at-risk youth.) (Headquarters, but missions are located in most cities.)
1045 Swift Street
Kansas City, MO 64116-4127
Phone: (816) 471-8020
Fax: (816) 471-3718
www.agrm.org

At the Door Program (Baltimore) (Has a special housing program for ex-offenders.)
417 East Fayette St.
Baltimore, MD 21202
Phone: (410) 396-3757
http://www.hero-mcrc.org/Services.htm

Conquest House (Conquest Offender Reintegration Ministry is an ex-offenders mentoring project that has a forthcoming transitioning housing and discipleship center.)
P.O. Box 73873
Washington, DC 20056-3873
Phone: (202) 723-2014
www.conquesthouse.org

The Corporation for Supportive Housing (CSH) (This national organization helps communities create permanent housing with services to prevent and end homelessness. CSH provides project-specific technical and financial assistance; the organization also works to build the capacity of the supportive housing industry and reform public policy to make it easier to create and operate supportive housing. Most of CSH's work takes place in the eight areas where they have local program offices: California, Illinois, Michigan, Minnesota, New Jersey, New York, Ohio, and Southern New England.)
www.csh.org

Delancey Street (Provides housing, education and work experience.)
600 Embarcadero
San Francisco, CA 94107
Phone: (415) 957-9800
http://www.grass-roots.org/usa/delancey.shtml

The Enterprise Foundation (This national organization assists nonprofits to develop affordable housing through their individualized technical assistance to community groups, as well as through online publications and products, trainings, funding, and public policy information. In housing development, they can assist with feasibility, planning, design, production, and management. Their assistance is available to groups in every state at a fee that varies on a case-by-case basis.)
www.enterprisefoundation.org

Exemplary Practices in Discharge Planning - PDF file Report and Recommendations of the Working Conference June 1997 The United States Interagency Council on Homelessness
451 7th Street, SW, Suite 2100
Washington, DC 20410
Phone: (202) 708-4663
Fax: (202) 708-1216
http://www.ich.gov/innovations/1/index.html
www.trosainc.org

The Fortune Academy (Staffed by ex-prisoners and is a public education organization that also helps ex-prisoners break the cycle of crime through a broad range of services.)
53 West 23rd Street, 8th Floor
New York, NY 10010
Phone: (212) 691-7554
Fax: (212) 255-4948
www.fortunesociety.org

The "Going Home" funding of reentry partnerships
The Serious and Violent Offender Initiative
http://www.ojp.usdoj.gov/reentry/whatsnew.html#regional
U.S. Department of Justice
Office of Justice Programs
http://www.ojp.usdoj.gov/reentry

Heritage Health and Housing (Provides housing to ex-prisoners and the homeless. Clients include people who have AIDS/HIV, mental illness, abuse substances.)
www.heritagehousing.org

Institutional Discharge and Homelessness
Summary of Recommendations
National Coalition for the Homeless
1012 Fourteenth Street, NW, #600
Washington, DC 20005-3471
Phone: (202) 737-6444
Fax: (202) 737-6445
http://www.nationalhomeless.org/health/institutional.html

Jericho Project (New York City) (Helps homeless people overcome substance abuse.)
891 Amsterdam Avenue
New York, NY 10025
Phone: (212) 316-4700
Fax: (212) 865-6554
www.jerichoproject.org

National Health Care for the Homeless Council, Inc.
HCH Clinicians' Network
P.O. Box 60427
Nashville, TN 37206-0427
Phone: (615) 226-2292
Fax: (615) 226-1656
http://www.nhchc.org/Advocacy/PolicyPapers
See National Health Care for the Homeless Recommendation
Summary Council 2003 Policy Statements "Institutional
Discharge and Homelessness"
http://www.nationalhomeless.org/health/institutional.html
http://www.nhchc.org/Advocacy/PolicyPapers/2003/07Insti
tutDischargen.pdf

Project Greenhope: Services for Women, Inc. (Works
with women who come out of the criminal justice system to
overcome substance abuse.)
448 E. 119th St.
New York, NY 10035-3626
Phone: (212) 369-5100
http://www.projectgreenhope.org/index.shtml

Public Safety Ex-Offender Self Sufficiency Act of 2002
News and Views
http://www.safer-fnd.org/news/1018991586.html

The Safer Foundation (Chicago) (Helps ex-offenders
make the transition back into the community.)
571 W. Jackson Blvd.
Chicago, IL 60661
Phone: (312) 922-2200
Fax: (312) 922-0839
www.safer-fnd.org

Saint Andrews Court, Project of St. Leonard's House
(Chicago)
2100 West Warren Blvd.
Chicago, IL 60612-2310
Phone: (312) 738-1414

Saint Stephens Catholic Church Ex-offender Housing Program (Assists ex-offenders to obtain housing, secure employment, and develop an action plan to successfully reenter society.)
2211 Clinton Avenue South
Minneapolis, MN 55404
Phone: (612) 874-0311
www.ststephenscommunity.org

Salvation Army
Phone: (703) 684-5500
www.salvationarmyusa.org

SPAN, Inc. (Boston) (Has a reintegration counseling program for state or county ex-offenders. They assist with housing, employment, and healthcare.)
110 Arlington Street
Boston, MA 02116
Phone: (617) 423-0750
Fax: (617) 482-2717

Strategies for Transitioning Ex-Offenders Program (STEP) Arizona Coalition to End Homelessness (Lists halfway houses, substance abuse treatment centers, health-care facilities, and employment services.)
http://www.azceh.org/attach/93_8e731e6763f31525275d8b83d6e3dd51.pdf

Triangle Residential Options for Substance Abusers, Inc
(TROSA) (Provides housing, substance treatment, and work
experience.)
1820 James Street
Durham, NC 27707
Phone: (919) 419-1059
www.trosainc.org

Volunteers of America (multiple sites in several states) (Is
a faith-based program that provides services to ex-offender.)
National Office
1660 Duke Street
Alexandria, VA 22314
Toll Free: (800) 899-0089
Phone: (703) 341-5000
Fax: (703) 341-7000
www.volunteersofamerica.org

Walden House (San Francisco and Los Angeles) (Works
with people who want to overcome substance abuse.)
520 Townsend Street
San Francisco, CA 94103
Phone: (415) 554-1100
www.waldenhouse.org

ARTICLES, BOOKS, AND VIDEOS

A *Guide to Developing Housing for People Living With HIV/AIDS* (Published in 2001 by Hudson Planning Group, this guide provides tools for those working to develop AIDS housing alternatives to low-quality commercial SRO housing. The guide includes descriptions and advice about questions to ask before you get started, phases of development, building a development team, developing the service model, selecting a site, design considerations, budgeting, federal and state sources of funding, and additional resources.) http://www.taclearinghouse.org/clearinghouse/resource.nsf/ $defaultView!OpenView

Breaking New Ground: Developing Innovative AIDS Care Residences (Published in 1993 and still the primary text on HIV/AIDS housing, *Breaking New Ground* leads potential housing developers through the steps of development from conceptualization through program evaluation, with case study examples from around the country.) www.aidshousing.org

Guide to Homeless Continuum of Care Planning and Implementation (Developed in collaboration with the National Supportive Housing Technical Assistance Partnership and published in 1999, the guide was designed as a training curriculum with collateral materials to assist communities in organizing, convening, and conducting a Continuum of Care planning process that is broadly inclusive and effective.) www.aidshousing.org

In My Backyard. Produced and directed by Corporation for Supportive Housing, 18 min., 1996, videocassette. www.csh.org. (Has a companion booklet: *Six Steps to*

Building Community Support.)

Mill, Manny and Jude Skallerup. *Radical Redemption: The Real Story of Manny Mill.* Moody Publications. (Mill is the founder of Koinonia House National Ministries, a post-prison ministry that helps bridge the gap from prison to the local church.)

National Law Center on Homelessness and Poverty. "Access Delayed, Access Denied: Local Opposition to Housing and Services for Homeless People Across the United States." Washington, D.C.: National Law Center on Homelessness and Poverty, December 1997.
http://www.aidshousing.org/ahw_library2275/ahw_library_show.htm?doc_id=35788

Placemakers: A Guide to Developing Housing for Homeless People (Published in 2000 by AIDS Housing of Washington and the HUD's Office of Special Needs Assistance Programs, this book is a compendium of presentations and materials gleaned from HUD's regional conferences on developing permanent housing for homeless people, which took place in Atlanta, Chicago, Dallas, Philadelphia, and San Francisco from February through April 2000.)
http://www.hud.gov/offices/cpd/homeless/library/place-makers/index.cfm

Proscio, Tony. *Forming an Effective Supportive Housing Consortium; Providing Services in Supportive Housing*; and *Developing and Managing Supportive Housing.* 2000. (These three manuals are designed to assist local communities and service and housing organizations to better understand the local planning consortium, service delivery and funding, and supportive housing development and financing.)
www.csh.org

Papers available online at www.csh.org from the Corporation for Supportive Housing: *An Overview of the Criminal Justice System, Project Financing Issues for Re-entry Supportive Housing, Guide to Re-entry Supportive Housing.*

Returning Home: Understanding the Challenges of Prisoner Reentry. (The Urban Institute released this brief on the findings of their study of prisoner reentry, Significantly, of the factors that returning inmates found useful in the first months after release, "church/mosque" (6.9%) ranked third behind "family" (20%) and "substance abuse treatment" (11%), and above "having a job" (6.2%), "social services" (4.8%), etc.)
http://www.urban.org/UploadedPDF/310946_BaltimorePris oners.pdf

Resources for Chapter 5: *"A Good Job"*

PRISON FELLOWSHIP PROGRAMS

Prison Fellowship
Prison Fellowship has produced excellent Aftercare training materials to assist churches in planning and developing their own ministries to ex-prisoners returning to their communities. PF will help the church customize its services according to the resources of its congregation and the needs of the community. Find out how to contact the nearest local Prison Fellowship office by calling toll-free (877) 478-0100.
National Office
P.O. Box 1550
Merrifield, VA 22116-1550
Phone: (703) 478-0100
www.prisonfellowship.org

The InnerChange Freedom Initiative (IFI) is a partnership between the state Department of Corrections and Prison Fellowship that prepares inmates for their return to society with the goal of reducing recidivism—through a 24-hour-a-day, 7-day-a-week values-based program taught from a biblical perspective. The in-prison phase is followed by a post-release phase that includes church involvement and mentoring. All prisoner participants volunteer for the program. IFI programs are currently operating in Texas, Iowa, Minnesota, and Kansas.
P.O. Box 1550
Merrifield, VA 22116-1550
Phone: (703) 478-0100 x 3729
www.ifiprison.org

Justice Fellowship, the criminal justice reform arm of Prison Fellowship, has a website with many issue papers, legislative updates, and resources related to prisoner reentry. While at the website please subscribe to the *Justice eReport*, a weekly e-mail update on criminal justice issues, legislation, and resources.
P.O. Box 1550
Merrifield, VA 22116-1550
Phone: (800) 217-2743
www.justicefellowship.org

PROGRAMS

Please note that while some of the following programs are state specific, they can be used as a helpful model.

The End Violence Project, "Getting a Job—Another Chance to Make It"
End Violence Project
511 N. Broad Street, Suite 604
Philadelphia, PA 19123
Phone: (610) 527-2821
www.endviolence.org

Identification/Driver's License See Parole Officer or Department of Motor Vehicles.

The MARO Employment and Training Association (A network of organizations that create opportunities for people with barriers to community access and employment.)
P.O. Box 16218
Lansing, MI 48901
Phone: (571) 484-5588
Fax: (571) 484-5411
http://www.doc.state.nc.us/rap

National Hire Network (Its goal is to increase the number and quality of job opportunities available to ex-offenders through changing public policies, employment practices, and public opinion.)
Legal Action Center
153 Waverly Place, 8th Floor
New York, NY 10014
Phone: (212) 243-1313
Fax: (212) 675-0286
www.hirenetwork.org

National Institute of Justice, National Institute of Corrections, Office of Corrections Education (Washington State's Corrections Clearinghouse: A Comprehensive Approach to Offender Employment)
National Institute of Justice
Washington, D.C.
Phone: (202) 307-2942
http://www.ncjrs.org/pdffiles1/174441.pdf

Project Return Milwaukee (Assists ex-offenders with employment, housing, and other needs.)
2821 N. 4th St., Suite 202
Milwaukee, WI 53212
Phone: (414) 374-8029
Fax: (414) 374-8033
www.projectreturnmilwaukee.org

Safer Foundation
Council to Reduce Recidivism Through Employment (C.A.R.R.E.)
571 West Jackson Blvd.
Chicago, IL 60661-5701
Phone: (312) 922-2200
http://www.safer-fnd.org/graphics/newsletter/fall01 reord.pdf

St. Joseph The Worker (Provides job placement and counseling.)
213 S. 11th Ave.
Phoenix, AZ 85002
Phone: (602) 257-4390
http://www.stjosephministry.org/index.html

Social Security Administration (Ex-prisoners will need a Social Security number to work.)
Phone: (800) 772-1213
www.ssa.gov

Union Gospel Mission
3211 Irving Blvd at Mockingbird
Dallas, TX 75211
Phone: (214) 637-6117
www.ugmdallas.org

U.S. Department of Labor Employment and Training Administration (Directs business, adults, youth, dislocated workers, and workforce professionals to training and employment services.)
U.S. Department of Labor
Frances Perkins Building
200 Constitution Avenue, NW
Washington, DC 20210
Phone: (877) 872-5681
www.doleta.gov

ARTICLES, BOOKS, AND VIDEOS

Buck, M. (2000). *Getting Back to Work: Employment Programs for Ex-Offenders*. Public Private Venture: Workforce Development. Finn, P. *Chicago's Safer Foundation: A Road Back for Exprisoners*. Washington, D.C.: U.S. Department of Justice, Office of Justice Programs, National Institute of Justice, 1998. NCJ 167575. http://www.ncjrs.org/pdffiles/167575.pdf

Finn, P. *Texas' Project RIO—Re-integration of Offenders, Program Focus*. Washington, D.C.: National Institute of Justice, n.d.

Houston, M. (2001). *Offender Job Retention*. National Institute of Corrections: Office of Correctional Job Training and Placement.

MacDonald, Heather. "Post-Prison Reform." *New York Post*, 15 June 2003.
http://www.manhattan-institute.org/html/_nypostpost_prison_reform.htm

Mendlin, Ronald, and Marc Polonsky. *Putting the Bars Behind You Workbook Series: A Job Preparation Guide Written Especially for Ex-prisoners*. Indianapolis: JIST Publishing, 2000. Available from JIST Publishing, 8902 Otis Avenue, Indianapolis, IN 46216; (800) 648-JIST. www.jist.com

Mukamal, D. (2001). *From Hard Time to Full Time: Strategies to Help Move Ex-Offenders from Welfare to Work*. U.S. Department of Labor: Employment and Training Administration.

O'Sullivan, K., N. Rose, and T. Murphy. "Connecting Juvenile Offenders to Education and Employment," *PEP Net: Fact Sheet*. Washington, D.C.: U.S. Department of Justice, Office of Justice Programs, Office of Juvenile Justice and Delinquency Prevention, 1997. NCJ 189558.
http://www.ncjrs.org/pdffiles1/ojjdp/fs200129.pdf

Prison Fellowship (Website article compiled by *Inside Journal,* which gives helpful pointers toward making a transition to employment.)
Phone: (703) 478-0100
http://www.pfm.org/Content/ContentGroups/Prison_Fellow
ship/Publications/Inside_Journal/Employment.htm

The Ex-inmate's Complete Guide to Successful Employment.
The Correctional Education Company and Aardvark Resumes & Career Counseling, 433 Franklin St., Patio Suite, Buffalo, NY 14202. "The Ex-offender Employment Task Force Report to the Illinois Workforce Investment Board" July 2002
http://www.ilworkforce.org/Docs/pdfs/IWIB/Aug2002/XOf
fenderFinalReport.PDF
The Legal Action Center has several publications for assisting returning offenders, including papers on housing, jobs and public assistance.
http://www.lac.org/pubs/gratis.html

"Path From Prison to a Job Gets More Attention in N.C.,"
The Associated Press, *NewsObserver.com*, 8 February 2004:
http://www.newsobserver.com/nc24hour/ncnews/
story/3315283p-2956769c.html
For more information contact:
North Carolina Department of Corrections
Office of Research and Planning
2020 Yonkers Road
4221 Mail Service Center
Raleigh, NC 27699-4221
Phone: (919) 716-3080
Fax: (919) 716-3990

U.S. Department of Labor Employment and Training Administration, "Strategies to Help Move Ex-Offenders from Welfare to Work: Appendices"; Appendix A: State Responses to the Drug Felon Ban; Appendix B: State Repositories of Criminal Records.
http://wtw.doleta.gov/documents/hard_appen.asp

Resources for Chapter 6: *"Access to Health Care"*

PRISON FELLOWSHIP PROGRAMS

Prison Fellowship
Prison Fellowship has produced excellent Aftercare and Mentoring training materials to assist churches in planning and developing their own ministries to ex-prisoners returning to their communities. PF will help the church customize its services according to the resources of its congregation and the needs of the community. Find out how to contact the nearest local Prison Fellowship office by calling toll-free (877) 478-0100.
National Office
P.O. Box 1550
Merrifield, VA 22116-1550
Phone: (703) 478-0100
www.prisonfellowship.org

The InnerChange Freedom Initiative (IFI) is a partnership between the state Department of Corrections and Prison Fellowship that prepares inmates for their return to society with the goal of reducing recidivism—through a 24-hour-a-day, 7-day-a-week values-based program taught from a biblical perspective. The in-prison phase is followed by a post-release phase that includes church involvement and mentoring. All prisoner participants volunteer for the program. IFI programs are currently operating in Texas, Iowa, Minnesota, and Kansas.
P.O. Box 1550
Merrifield, VA 22116-1550
Phone: (703) 478-0100 x 3729
www.ifiprison.org

Justice Fellowship, the criminal justice reform arm of Prison Fellowship, has a website with many issue papers, legislative updates, and resources related to prisoner reentry. While at the website please subscribe to the *Justice eReport*, a weekly e-mail update on criminal justice issues, legislation, and resources.
P.O. Box 1550
Merrifield, VA 22116-1550
Phone: (800) 217-2743
www.justicefellowship.org

Programs
The Bazelon Center for Mental Health Law
1101 15th Street, NW
Suite 1212
Washington, DC 20005
Phone: (202) 467-5730
Fax: (202) 223-0409
www.bazelon.org

Center for Mental Health Services
Knowledge Exchange Network
P.O. Box 42490
Washington, DC 20015
Phone: (800) 789-2647
www.mentalhealth.org

Emotions Anonymous (A 12-step organization composed of people who come together weekly to work toward recovery from emotional difficulties.)
P.O. Box 4245
St. Paul, MN 55104
Phone: (651) 647-9712
www.emotionsanonymous.org

National Alliance for the Mentally Ill
200 North Glebe Road, Suite 1015
Arlington, VA 22203-3754
Phone: (703) 524-7600
www.nami.org

National Commission on Correctional Health Care
1300 W. Belmont Ave.
Chicago, IL 60657
Phone: (773) 880-1460
Fax: (773) 880-2424
www.ncchc.org

The National GAINS Center for People with Co-Occurring Disorders in the Justice System Policy Research Associates, Inc. (Offers materials and information about the best mental-health and substance abuse practices and programs around the country.)
345 Delaware Avenue
Delmar, NY 12054
Phone: (800) 311-4246
Fax: (518) 439-7612
www.gainsctr.com

National Institute of Corrections Community Corrections Division
500 1st Street, 7th Floor
Washington, DC 20534
Phone: (800) 995-6423
http://www.nicic.org/resources/topics/TransitionFromPrison.aspx

Project Bridge (Provides outreach and reentry case management, and medical follow-up for ex-prisoners.)
369 Broad Street
Providence, RI 02907
Phone: (401) 455-6879

U.S. Department of Health and Human Services
Substance Abuse and Mental Health Services Administration
Room 12-105 Parklawn Building
5600 Fishers Lane
Rockville, MD 20857
Phone: (301) 443-0001 (Center for Mental Health Services)
www.samhsa.gov

ARTICLES, BOOKS, AND VIDEOS

Barr, Heather. *How to Help When a Person with Mental Illness is Arrested: A New York City Handbook for Family, Friends, Advocates, and Mental Health Workers.*
New York: The Open Society Institute, March 2001.
Bernstein, Robert. "For People with Serious Mental Illnesses: Finding the Key to Successful Transition From Jail to the Community, An Explanation of Federal Medicaid and Disability Program Rules."
http://www.bazelon.org/issues/criminalization/findingthekey.html

The Courage to Change: A Guide for Communities to Create Integrated Services for People with Co-Occurring Disorders in the Justice System. Delmar, N.Y.: The GAINS Center. December 1999.
http://www.gainsctr.com/pdfs/monographs/CourageToChange.pdf

"Criminal Justice/Mental Health Consensus Project of the Council of State Governments" (The Criminal Justice/Mental Health Consensus Project is an national effort to help local, state, and federal policymakers and criminal justice and mental health professionals improve the response to people with mental illness who become involved in, or are at risk of involvement in, the criminal justice system.)
http://consensusproject.org/topics/toc

Hammett, T.M., C. Roberts, and S. Kennedy. "Health related Issues in Prisoner Reentry." *Crime & Delinquency* 47, no. 3. (July 2001): 390-409. NCJ 188919.

"The Health Status of Soon-to-be-Released Inmates: A Report of Congress." National Commission on Correctional Health Care. There are two volumes.
http://www.ncchc.org/stbr/Volume1/Health%20Status%20(vol%201).pdf
http://www.ncchc.org/stbr/Volume2/Health%20Status%20(vol%202).pdf

Holmes, Leah (project director). Case Study: Project Bridge. Health & Disability Working Group Boston University School of Public Health.
http://www.bu.edu/hdwg/projects/trainingfiles/ProjectBridge.pdf

"Involving Families in Systems Change: Improving Services for People with Co-Occurring Disorders in the Criminal and Juvenile Justice System," The GAINS Center.
http://www.gainsctr.com/pdfs/brochures/Involving_Families_Prov.pdf

McGughey, Christmas. "Experts: Sick Prisoners Could Endanger Public." *Mobile Register*, 25 September 2003.
http://www.al.com/news/mobileregister/index.ssf?/base/news/106448150093420.xml

National Healthcare for the Homeless Council (2003 Policy Statements) Institutional Discharge and Homelessness Range, Stacey.

"State Creates Hepatitis C Panel. Group to Look at Testing, Treating of Prison Inmates." *Lansing State Journal*, October 1, 2003
http://www.lsj.com/news/local/031001hepc_1a-4a.html.
See also Range, Stacey. "Hepatitis C in Prisons Worries Guards." *Lansing State Journal*. September 30, 2003.
http://www.lsj.com/news/local/030930guards_hepc_1a-4a.html

"Report Finds Mistreatment and Neglect of Mentally Ill in Prisons." Human Rights Watch. 22 October 2003.
www.hrw.org/press/2003/10/us102203.htm.
See report www.hrw.org/reports/2003/usa1003

Strickland, Ted. "Office of Correctional Health." H.R. 1993, May 6, 2003. http://frwebgate.access.gpo.gov/cgi-bin/get doc.cgi?dbname=108_cong_bills&docid=f:h1993ih.txt.pdf. See also "Mentally Ill Offender Treatment and Crime Reduction Act of 2003." S. 1194. http://thomas.loc.gov/ cgibin/query/F?c108:4:./temp/~c108wXMVA0:e615

Wahlberg, David. "Staph Outbreak Plagues Prisons." *The Atlanta Journal-Constitution* 17 October 2003. http:// www.ajc.com/news/content/news/1003/17staph.html;COXn etJSessionID=1PiHI2EWGOWWi1cqjTe1feQ1P8kqeskyItp L0Cw6bc1PkfaaNLwj!373615475?urac=n&urvf=1066394 1839120.8243187018886978

Zeilbuer, Paul von. "Report on New York Prisons Cites Inmates' Mental Illness." The *New York Times*, October 22, 2003
http://query.nytimes.com/gst/abstract.html?res=FA061EFE 3D550C718EDDA90994DB404482

Zeilbuer, Paul von. "Mentally Ill Inmates Discarding Medicine Pose Problem." *New York Times*, October 27, 2003.
http://query.nytimes.com/gst/abstract.html?res=F30F1FFD
3A550C748EDDA90994DB404482

Resources for Chapter 7: *"Freedom from Addiction"*

PRISON FELLOWSHIP PROGRAMS

Prison Fellowship

Prison Fellowship has produced excellent Aftercare training materials to assist churches in planning and developing their own ministries to ex-prisoners returning to their communities. PF also has a Christ-centered seminar called "Free At Last," which deals with breaking free from addictive and compulsive behaviors. PF will help the church customize its services according to the resources of its congregation and the needs of the community. Find out how to contact the nearest local Prison Fellowship office by calling toll-free (877) 478-0100.
National Office
P.O. Box 1550
Merrifield, VA 22116-1550
Phone: (703) 478-0100
www.prisonfellowship.org

The InnerChange Freedom Initiative (IFI) is a partnership between the state Department of Corrections and Prison Fellowship that prepares inmates for their return to society with the goal of reducing recidivism—through a 24-hour-a-day, 7-day-a-week values-based program taught from a biblical perspective. The in-prison phase is followed by a post-release phase that includes church involvement

and mentoring. All prisoner participants volunteer for the program. IFI programs are currently operating in Texas, Iowa, Minnesota, and Kansas.
P.O. Box 1550
Merrifield, VA 22116-1550
Phone: (703) 478-0100 x 3729
www.ifiprison.org

Justice Fellowship, the criminal justice reform arm of Prison Fellowship, has a website with many issue papers, legislative updates, and resources related to prisoner reentry. While at the website please subscribe to the *Justice eReport*, a weekly e-mail update on criminal justice issues, legislation, and resources.
P.O. Box 1550
Merrifield, VA 22116-1550
Phone: (800) 217-2743
www.justicefellowship.org

GENERAL INFORMATION ON REENTRY AND ADDICTION

The National Center on Addiction and Substance Abuse at Columbia University (CASA)
633 Third Avenue, 19th Floor
New York, NY 10017-6706
Phone: (212) 841-5200
www.casacolumbia.org

U.S. Department of Health and Human Services
Substance Abuse and Mental Health Services Administration
Rm 12-105 Parklawn Building
5600 Fishers Lane
Rockville, MD 20857
Phone: (301) 443-5700 (Center for Substance Abuse Treatment)

You may obtain information about SAMHSA's Young Offender Reentry Program and download application materials at http://www.samhsa.gov/grants/grants.html

Vera Institute of Justice
Phone: (212) 334-1300
Fax: (212) 941-9407
www.vera.org

Support for Drug-Abusing Offenders and Their Families
http://www.vera.org/project/project1_1.asp?section_id=3&project_id=23&archive=NO

Prison-Based Drug Treatment for Parole Violators
http://www.vera.org/project/project1_1.asp?section_id=3&project_id=44&archive=NO

PROGRAMS

Addicts Victorious
639 York Street, Suite #210
Quincy, IL 62301-3919
Phone: (217) 223-1388
Fax: (217) 223-4870
E-Mail: victory@addictsvictorious.com
Hotline: (800) 323-1388 • Quincy (217) 222-7077
www.addictsvictorious.com

Al-Anon/Alateen (Program offers support for family members and friends of someone with a drinking problem.)

Al-Anon/Alateen Family Group
World Service Office
1600 Corporate Landing Pkwy.
Virginia Beach, VA 23454-56517
Phone: (800) 356-9996
www.ct-al-anon.org

Alcoholics Anonymous (AA) (Fellowship of people who encourage one another in sobriety.)
P.O. Box 459
Grand Central Station
New York, NY 10163
Phone: (212) 870-3400
www.alcoholics-anonymous.org

Alcoholics Victorious
Phone: (816) 471-8020
www.alcoholicsvictorious.org

The Bowery Mission Transitional Center
45-51 Avenue D
New York, NY 10009
Phone: (800) 869-3791
http://www.bowery.org

Celebrate Recovery (Christ-centered program based on 8 Recovery Principles to break free of addictive and compulsive behaviors.)
Phone: (949) 609-8305
www.celebraterecovery.com

Gospel Rescue Mission (Provides emergency food and shelter, youth and family services, rehabilitation programs for the addicted; education and job training programs and assistance to the elderly poor and at-risk youth.) (Headquarters, but missions are located in most cities.)
1045 Swift Street
Kansas City, MO 64116-4127
Phone: (816) 471-8020
Fax: (816) 471-3718
http://www.agrm.org

La Bodega de La Familia
272 East Third Street
NYC, NY 10009
Phone: (212) 982-2335

Narcotics Anonymous (Community-based association of recovering drug addicts.)
P.O. Box 9999
Van Nuys, CA 91409
Phone: (818) 773-9999
www.na.org

The National GAINS Center for People with Co-Occurring Disorders in the Justice System Policy Research Associates, Inc. (Offers materials and information about the best mental-health and substance abuse practices and programs around the country.)
345 Delaware Avenue
Delmar, NY 12054
Phone: (800)-311-4246
Fax: (518) 439-7612
http://www.gainsctr.com

New Life Ministries
P.O. Box 866997
Plano, TX 75086
Phone: (800) NEW-LIFE (639-5433)
www.newlife.com/calvary.html

Overcomers Outreach (Ministry dealing with all compulsive behaviors through Christ-centered 12-step support groups.)
P.O. Box 2208
Oakhurst, CA 93644
Phone: (800) 310-3001
www.overcomersoutreach.org

Rapha Christian Counseling
Irving, Texas
Phone: (800) 383-HOPE
www.rapha.info/index.html
Also see chapter four on *"A Safe Place to Live"* because many housing programs also offer treatment for substance abuse.

The Rebecca Project for Human Rights
1752 Columbia Road, NW, Third Floor
Washington, DC 20009
Phone: (202) 265-3907
www.rebeccaproject.org/cross.php

The Salvation Army Adult Rehabilitation Centers
(Christian organization providing shelter, food, clothing, medical and psychiatric assistance, work, vocational training, fellowship, and spiritual guidance.)
P.O. Box 269
Alexandria, VA 22313
Phone: (703) 684-5500
www.salvationarmyusa.org

The Spirit of Freedom Ministries (Christian organization dedicated to helping prisoners and families end their alcohol or drug-related problems.)
P.O. Box 6684
Metairie, LA 70009-6648
Phone: (800) 535-6011
www.sofm.org

Teen Challenge International, USA (Faith-based substance-abuse prevention and treatment program, which has multiple centers worldwide.)
3728 W. Chestnut Expressway
Springfield, MO 65802
Phone: (417) 862-6969
www.teenchallenge.com

Treatment Alternatives for Safe Communities (TASC)
Administrative Offices
1500 N. Halsted
Chicago, IL 60622
Phone: (312) 787-0208
Fax: (312) 787-9663
http://www.tasc-il.org/preview/clients.html

ARTICLES, BOOKS, AND VIDEOS

Alexander, Robert B., Pratsinak, George J. *Arresting Addictions: Drug Education and Relapse Prevention.* American Correctional Association, 2002.
http://www.aca.org/bookstore/view.asp?product_id=290&origin=results&QS='&YMGHFREkey_words=Substance+Abuse&pagesize=10&top_parent=257

Cullen, Murray C., Bradley, Michael. *Inside/Out: Continuing to Cage Your Rage* (An Inmate's Guide to Anger Control). American Correctional Association, 2001.
http://www.aca.org/bookstore/view.asp?product_id=271&origin=results&QS='&YMGHFREkey_words=Anger+Management&pagesize=10&pg=2&top_parent=257

Gorski, Terence. "Counselor's Manual for Relapse Prevention with Chemically Dependent Criminal Offenders." *Technical Assistance Publications,* No. 19. U.S. Department of Health and Human Services, n.d.
www.treatment.org/TAPS/TAP19/TAP19.html

Kassebaum, Patricia. "Substance Abuse Treatment for Women Offenders: Guide to Promising Practices." *Technical Assistance Duplication Series,* No. 23. Washington, D.C.: U.S. Department of Health and Human Services, 1999.
http://www.treatment.org/Taps/Tap23.pdf

Successfully Housing People with Substance Use Issues (SHPSUI) (Developed in conjunction with the Corporation for Supportive Housing, the SHPSUI training guide comprises a training curriculum and collateral materials that target front-line workers in AIDS and supportive housing programs and offers experience- based tools and strategies to increase housing stability and build successful resident communities among this challenging tenant population.)
www.csh.org

The National GAINS Center for People with Co-Occurring Disorders in the Justice System. *The Courage to Change: A Guide for Communities to Create Integrated Services for People with Co-Occurring Disorders in the Justice System.* Delmar, NY
National GAINS Center for People with Co-Occurring Disorders in the Justice System, December 1999.
http://www.gainsctr.com/pdfs/monographs/CourageToChange.pdf

Resources for Chapter 8: *"Repairing the Harm Done by Crime"*

PRISON FELLOWSHIP PROGRAMS

Prison Fellowship
Prison Fellowship has produced excellent Aftercare and Mentoring training materials to assist churches in planning and developing their own ministries to ex-prisoners returning to their communities. PF will help the church customize its services according to the resources of its congregation and the needs of the community. Find out how to contact the nearest local Prison Fellowship office by calling toll-free (877) 478-0100.
National Office
P.O. Box 1550
Merrifield, VA 22116-1550
Phone: (703) 478-0100
www.prisonfellowship.org

Angel Tree® is Prison Fellowship's ministry to children of prisoners, working in partnership with thousands of churches throughout the United States. It includes three programs: Angel Tree Christmas, which provides Christmas gifts and the Gospel message to prisoners' children; Angel Tree Camping, where churches sponsor prisoners' children to attend Christ-centered summer camps; and Angel Tree Mentoring, in which churches match prisoners' children in long-term one-to-one relationships with caring Christian adults.
P.O. Box 1550
Merrifield, VA 22116-1550
Phone: (800) 552-6435
www.angeltree.org

The InnerChange Freedom Initiative (IFI) is a partnership between the state Department of Corrections and Prison Fellowship that prepares inmates for their return to society with the goal of reducing recidivism—through a 24-hour-a-day, 7-day-a-week values-based program taught from a biblical perspective. The in-prison phase is followed by a post-release phase that includes church involvement and mentoring. All prisoner participants volunteer for the program. IFI programs are currently operating in Texas, Iowa, Minnesota, and Kansas.
P.O. Box 1550
Merrifield, VA 22116-1550
Phone: (703) 478-0100 x 3729
www.ifiprison.org

Justice Fellowship, the criminal justice reform arm of Prison Fellowship, has a website with many issue papers, legislative updates, and resources related to prisoner reentry and Restorative Justice. While at the website please subscribe to the *Justice eReport*, a weekly e-mail update on criminal justice issues, legislation, and resources.
P.O. Box 1550
Merrifield, VA 22116-1550
Phone: (800) 217-2743
www.justicefellowship.org

Prison Fellowship International Centre for Justice and Reconciliation
Restorative Justice OnLine at www.restorativejustice.org has numerous resources on Restorative Justice, both in theory and in practice, from around the globe, as well as links to other Restorative Justice resources.
P.O. Box 17434
Washington, DC 20041
www.restorativejustice.org

PROGRAMS FOR VICTIMS AND RESTORATIVE JUSTICE

Center for Peacemaking and Conflict Studies
Fresno Pacific University
1717 S. Chestnut Ave. #2202
Fresno, CA 93702
Phone: (559) 455-5840
Fax: (559) 252-4800
Toll-free: (800) 909-8677
e-mail: pacs@fresno.edu
www.fresno.edu/pacs

Conflict Transformation Program
Eastern Mennonite University
1200 Park Road
Harrisonburg, VA 22802-2462
Phone: (540) 432-4000
Fax: (540) 432-4444
www.emu.edu/ctp/ctp.html

Criminal Justice Chaplaincy (Provides church and community outreach services and ministers to individuals, families, and groups involved in the criminal justice system.)
345 State Street, SE
Grand Rapids, MI 49503-4349
Phone: (616) 454-4925
Fax: (616) 454-8835
www.crcjustice.org/crjs_restore_chaplaincy.htm

The Justice and Reconciliation Project (Works to bring restoration, reconciliation, and healing to crime victims and offenders, and to raise up a victims-led voice in support of Restorative Justice policies.)
P.O. Box 366
Smartville, CA 95977
Phone: (530) 639-2668
Fax: (530) 639-2668
Lisa Rea, Founder and President, lrea@mindsync.com
http://www.thejrp.org/

La Bodega de La Familia
272 East Third Street
New York, NY 10009
Phone: (212) 982-2335

National Organization for Victim Assistance
1730 Park Road, NW
Washington, DC 20010
Phone: (202) 232-6682
www.try-nova.org

National Organization for Victims Rights
1730 Park Road, NW
Washington, DC 20010
Phone: (800) 879-6682, (202) 232-6682
Fax: 462-2255
www.trynova.org/contact.html

OASIS (Interactive website that offers crime victims step-by-step instructions to post and/or retrieve meaningful information about their case.)
P.O. Box 30856
Lincoln, NE 68510
Phone: (402) 429-105
www.oasis-ne.org

Office for Victims of Crime, U.S. Department of Justice
810 7th Street, NW
Washington, DC 20531
www.ojp.usdoj.gov/ovc/welcome.html

Office of Justice Programs, U.S. Department of Justice
(Material on programs about victim-offender reconciliation.)
810 Seventh Street, NW
Washington, DC 20001
Phone: (202) 307-5933
Publications: Victim Assistance Community: Mediation
www.ojp.usdoj.gov/ovc/publications/infores/pubguide_01_01/pubres_19g.html

Opening Doors (Partnership between Ohio's churches and prisons that teaches inmates how to resolve conflicts. It is designed by Debbie Roeger, an attorney and mediator, who combined her professional skills with biblical principles to create this excellent program.)
Opening Doors of Ohio, Inc.
P.O. Box 281
Lewis Center, OH 43035-9281
Phone: (740) 363-4227, (614) 361-6783
OpeningDoors@columbus.rr.com

Restorative Justice Ministry Network of North America
1232 Avenue J
Huntsville, TX 77340
Phone: (936) 291-2156
http://66.96.187.49/welcome.htm

Victim Offender Mediation Association (VOMA) (An international membership association that supports and assists people and communities working at restorative models of justice.)
c/o Center for Policy, Planning and Performance
2344 Nicollet Avenue South, Suite 330
Minneapolis, MN 55404
Phone: (612) 874-0570
Fax: (612) 874-0253
http://voma.org

Victim-Offender Reconciliation Program Information and Resource Center (VORP) (Brings offenders face-to-face with the victims of their crimes with the assistance of a trained mediator.)
1007 NE 118th Avenue
Portland, OR 97220
Phone: (503) 255-8677
www.vorp.com

ARTICLES, BOOKS, AND VIDEOS ON VICTIMS

American Bar Association Endorsement of Victim-Offender Mediation/Dialogue Programs. August 1994. www.vorp.com/articles/abaendors.html

Bellard, Jan. "Victim Offender Mediation." *The Community Mediator.* Fall 2000. http://voma.org/docs/bellard.pdf

Bloom, Barbara and David Steinhart. *Why Punish the Children: A Reappraisal of the Children of Incarcerated Mothers in America*, San Francisco, 1993.

Coates, R. and J. Gehm (1985). "Victim Meets Offender: An Evaluation of Victim-Offender Reconciliation Programs." Valparaiso, IN: PACT Institute of Justice;

Coates, R. and J. Gehm (1989). "An Empirical Assessment" in M. Wright and B. Galaway (eds.) *Mediation and Criminal Justice.* London: Sage, pp. 251-263. This is one of the first empirical studies in the U.S. to assess Victim-Offender Reconciliation Programs (VORP). http://ssw.che.umn.edu/rjp/Resources/Documents/RJAnnotated%20Bib.pdf

Edmunds, Leah. "La Bodega Wins Innovations in American Government Award." *Just 'Cause*, Vera Institute of Justice, Vol. 10, No. 2, March/April 2003.

Kuecker, Thomas, Chun-Hao Li, Chris Maxwell, Lori Post, and Carl S. Taylor. *Services to Enable and Empower Kids.* (Project SEEK) Public Policy Briefing Report, Institute for Children, Youth, and Families, 1999.

Price, Marty. "Personalizing Crime: Mediation Produces Restorative Justice for Victims and Offenders." *Dispute Resolution Magazine.* Fall 2001. www.vorp.com/articles/justice.html

Price, Marty. "Crime and Punishment: Can Mediation Produce Restorative Justice for Victims and Offenders?" Victim-Offender Reconciliation Program Information and Resource Center. www.vorp.com/articles/crime.html

"Responsibility, Rehabilitation, and Restoration: A Catholic Perspective on Crime and Criminal Justice," A Statement of the Catholic Bishops of the United States www.usccb.org/sdwp/criminal.htm

Umbreit, M.S., *Family Group Conferencing: Implications for Crime Victims, 2000.* Washington, D.C.: U.S. Department of Justice, Office of Justice Programs, Office for Victims of Crime, April 2000. NCJ 176347. www.ojp.usdoj.gov/ovc/publications/infores/restorative_justice

Umbreit, Mark, et.al. *Victim Meets Offender: The Impact of Restorative Justice and Mediation.* Monsey, NY: Criminal Justice Press, 1994.

Wells, Martin. "Ex-Convict Brings Criminals, Victims Together, on the Internet." Voice of America. 17 January 2003.
www.voanews.com

PROGRAMS FOR FAMILIES OF OFFENDERS

The Administration for Children and Families (ACF) of the Department of Health and Human Services has a website with much information about programs for children and families: www.acf.hhs.gov/
It is also the federal agency managing the **Children of Prisoners Initiative**. The following link is to the ACF press release that gives a "barebones" description of the program: www.acf.hhs.gov/news/press/2003/release_052003.html

AIM, Inc. Aid to Inmate Mothers (AIM) (Project Reconnect helps pre-released women set life goals and become oriented to life outside prison walls. They work with post-released women for job placement, housing, and counseling. Participants receive at least one year follow-up.)
www.inmatemoms.org/reconnect.htm

Caliber Associates (Provides research and consulting services that help clients develop and manage effective human service programs and policies for the public good.)
10530 Rosehaven Street, Suite 400
Fairfax, VA 22030
Phone: (703) 385-3200
www.caliber.com

The Center for Fathers, Families, and Workforce Development (A six-week program for incarcerated fathers focusing on child support issues.)
3002 Druid Park Drive
Baltimore, MD 21215
(410) 367-5691

Child Welfare League of America (Promotes the well-being of children and protecting them from harm.)
440 First Street, NW, Third Floor
Washington, DC 20001-2085
Phone: (202) 638-2952
Fax: (202) 638-4004
www.cwla.org

Families in Crisis
30 Arbor Street North Wing
Hartford, CT 06106
Phone: (860) 236-3595
Fax: (860) 231-8430
www.familiesincrisis.org

Family and Corrections Network (FCN) (publishes *FCN REPORT*, the only national publication devoted to families of prisoners.)
32 Oak Grove Road
Palmyra, VA 22963
Phone: (434) 589-3036
Fax: (434) 589-6520
www.fcnetwork.org

Family Justice, Inc. (Helps families work effectively together to build healthy relationships that improve ex-offenders' successful transition into family and community life.)
625 Broadway, 8th Floor
New York, NY 10012
Phone: (212) 475-1500
Fax: (212) 475-2322
www.familyjusticeinc.org

Family Reentry (Assists fathers who have become disconnected from children through incarceration to become more positively involved parents. It works to increase their skills in nurturing, discipline, and socializing children appropriately.)
9 Mott Avenue, Suite 104
Norwalk, CT 06850
Phone: (203) 838-0496
www.familyreentry.org/fathers_prog.html

The Father's Workshop, Long Distance Dads (Albion, Pennsylvania) (Provides training and curricula for anyone working with fathers who are being released from prison.)
www.thefathersworkshop.org

Fathers and Families Together (FAFT) (Develops programs related to fatherhood and healthy families.)
6001 Woodland Avenue
Cleveland, OH 44108
Phone: (216) 432-7200 x 204
www.c4fc.org/programs/fathers___families.html

Institute for Children, Youth, and Families (ICYF at Michigan State University is a multidisciplinary institute supporting university-community collaboration in research, outreach, and policy analysis to improve the lives of children, youth, and families from diverse communities.)
Michigan State University
Suite 27 Kellogg Center
East Lansing, MI 48824
Phone: (517) 353-6617
Fax: (517) 432-2022
www.icyf.msu.edu

Justice Works
1012 Eight Avenue
Brooklyn, NY 11215
Phone: (718) 499-6704
Fax: (718) 832-2932
www.justiceworks.org

The Mentoring Center (Promotes, develops, and implements the concept of mentoring youth from all backgrounds.)
1221 Preservation Park Way, Suite 200
Oakland, CA 94512
Phone: (510) 891-0427
Fax: (510) 891-0492
www.mentor.org

The National Fatherhood Initiative
101 Lake Forest Blvd., Suite 360
Gaithersburg, MD 20877
Phone: (301) 948-0599
Fax: (301) 948-4325
www.fatherhood.org

National Mentoring Center (Provides helpful information on how to start a youth mentoring program.)
Northwest Regional Educational Laboratory
101 S.W. Main Street, Suite 500
Portland, OR 97204
Phone: (800) 5457-6339
Fax: (503) 275-0135
www.nwrel.org/mentoring/topic_startup.html

Papas and Their Children (This San Antonio, Texas, jail-based education program for fathers focuses on child support, parenting, nutrition, anger management, and behavior modification.)
Phone: (210) 335-6330
See "Support Services for Incarcerated and Released NonCustodial Parents," Heidi Sachs, *Welfare Information Services*, Vol. 4, No. 6.
www.welfareinfo.org/heidijune2.htm

The Rebecca Project for Human Rights (A legal and policy advocacy organization for poor and low-income families struggling with intersecting issues of substance abuse, access to family-oriented treatment, the criminal justice system and economic marginality.)
1752 Columbia Road, NW, Third Floor
Washington, DC 20009
Phone: (202) 265-3907
www.rebeccaproject.org/cross.php

ARTICLES, BOOKS, AND VIDEOS ON FAMILIES OF OFFENDERS

Boyce, Daniel J. *As Free as a Eagle: The Inmate's Family Survival Guide*. American Correctional Association, 1993. (Self-help guide teaches offenders how to establish productive relationships, develop problem-solving skills, and reenter society upon release.)

The Center for Children of Incarcerated Parents (CCIP's mission is the prevention of intergenerational crime and incarceration.)
www.e-ccip.org

Children's Services Practice Notes Newsletter (This is a newsletter sponsored by the North Carolina Division of Social Services and the N.C. Family and Children's Resource Program and has a great overview of the issues related to the topic.)
http://ssw.unc.edu/fcrp/cspn/vol7_no1.htm

Colson, Charles W. *Justice that Restores*. Wheaton, IL: Tyndale House Publishers, 2001.
Department of Health and Human Services (Announces grants for Mentoring Children of Prisoners.)
www.dol.gov/cfbci/funding.htm#hhsgrant
See also http://a257.g.akamaitech.net/7/257/2422/14mar 20010800/edocket.access.gpo.gov/ 2004/04-3844.htm

Gadsden, Vivian L. *Heading Home: Offender Reintegration into the Family*. American Correctional Association, 2003.
www.aca.org/bookstore/view.asp?product_id=359&origin= results&QS='&YMGHFREproduct_name=heading+home &pagesize=10&top_parent=257

Gaseau, Michelle. "Supporting Children with Incarcerated Parents Through Partnerships." *Corrections.com.* 2 February 2004. http://database.corrections.com/news/results2.asp?ID=9489

Grossman, Jean Baldwin and Eileen M. Garry. "Mentoring—A Proven Delinquency Prevention Strategy," *Juvenile Justice Bulletin*, April 1997. www.ncjrs.org/pdffiles/164834.pdf

Information Technology International. *Evaluating Your Program: A Beginner's Self-Evaluation Workbook for Mentoring Programs* http://itiincorporated.com/sew_dl.htm

Jeffries, John. *Serving Incarcerated and Ex-Offender Fathers and Their Families: A Review of The Field* (monograph). New York: Vera Institute of Justice and Charles Stewart Mott Foundation, February 2001. Online: http://www.vera.org/publication_pdf/fathers.pdf

Legal Services for Prisoners with Children (LSPC advocates for the civil rights and empowerment of incarcerated parents, children, family members, and people at risk for incarceration. Focus is on women prisoners and their families and has strong legal advocacy content. Several publications and extensive links might help in framing issues.) http://prisonerswithchildren.org

Life Recovery-Women Empowering Women www.liferecoveryprogram.org

National Institute of Corrections: Children of Prisoners Videoconference June 18, 2003. (This three-hour videoconference will identify the problems and greatest needs of

incarcerated parents and caretakers with regard to their children. This conference is late in the game from the grant writing perspective but might have information that informs the final draft of your proposal.)
www.nicic.org/services/video/03-children.htm

National Institute of Corrections: "Women Arise — A Day Reporting Center," Detroit, MI
www.nicic.org/pubs/2001/016735.pdf

Oakland Press, April 13, 2003, "Experts: Families Vital to Prisoners' Rehabilitation." Public/Private Ventures: Contemporary Issues in Mentoring.
http://ppv.org/content/ reports/issuesinmentoring.html
See also, Making a Difference: An Impact Study of Big Brothers/Big Sisters.
http://ppv.org/content/reports/makingadiff.html

Sachs, Heidi. "Support Services for Incarcerated and Released Non-Custodial Parents." *Welfare Information Network Issue Notes* 4, no. 6 (June 2000).
www.welfareinfo.org/heidijune2.htm

Saker, Annie. "Inmates, Kids Tighten Bonds: Camp Unites Children, Imprisoned Fathers to Play, Create, Connect." *Newsobserver.com*. 28 March 2004.
http://newsobserver.com/news/nc/story/3458155p-3073897c.html

Support for Drug-Abusing Offenders and Their Families
www.vera.org/project/project1_1.asp?section_id=3&project_id=23&archive=NO
www.cor.state.pa.us/families.pdf

Van Ness, Daniel W. and Karen Heetderks Strong. *Restoring Justice*, second edition. Cincinnati, OH: Anderson Publishing, 2002.

Van Ness, Daniel W. *Crime and Its Victims: What We Can Do*. Downers Grove, IL: InterVarsity Press, 1986.

Zehr, Howard. *Changing Lenses: A New Focus for Crime and Justice*. Scottdale, PA: Herald Press, 1990.

Resources for Chapter 9: *"Restoring the Community"*

PRISON FELLOWSHIP PROGRAMS

Prison Fellowship
Prison Fellowship has produced excellent Aftercare and Mentoring training materials to assist churches in planning and developing their own ministries to ex-prisoners returning to their communities. PF will help the church customize its services according to the resources of its congregation and the needs of the community. Find out how to contact the nearest local Prison Fellowship office by calling toll-free (877) 478-0100.
National Office
P.O. Box 1550
Merrifield, VA 22116-1550
Phone: (703) 478-0100
www.prisonfellowship.org

The InnerChange Freedom Initiative (IFI) is a partnership between the state Department of Corrections and Prison Fellowship that prepares inmates for their return to society with the goal of reducing recidivism—through a 24-

hour-a-day, 7-day-a-week values-based program taught from a biblical perspective. The in-prison phase is followed by a post-release phase that includes church involvement and mentoring. All prisoner participants volunteer for the program. IFI programs are currently operating in Texas, Iowa, Minnesota, and Kansas.
P.O. Box 1550
Merrifield, VA 22116-1550
Phone: (703) 478-0100 x 3729
www.ifiprison.org

Justice Fellowship, the criminal justice reform arm of Prison Fellowship, has a website with many issue papers, legislative updates, and resources related to prisoner reentry. While at the website please subscribe to the *Justice eReport*, a weekly e-mail update on criminal justice issues, legislation, and resources.
P.O. Box 1550
Merrifield, VA 22116-1550
Phone: (800) 217-2743
www.justicefellowship.org

GENERAL RESOURCES ON COMMUNITY RESTORATION

Community Justice Institute
Florida Atlantic University
111 East Las Olas Blvd
Askew Tower, Suite 613
Ft. Lauderdale FL, 33304
Phone: (954) 762-5668
Fax: (954) 762-5626
http://www.fau.edu/divdept/caupa/centers/cji/overview.html

Transition of Prisoners works to encourage, train, and support local churches in building their capacity to more effectively minister to prisoners, ex-prisoners in transition, and their families.
P.O. Box 02938
Detroit, MI 48202
(313) 875-3883
www.topinc.net/index.htm

PROGRAMS FOR COMMUNITY RESTORATION

Center for Restorative Justice & Peacemaking, University of Minnesota—School of Social Work center dedicated to the development of community-based responses to violence and crime, and training for professionals and community volunteers in corrections and victim services; program descriptions, publications, and general information.
Center for Restorative Justice & Peacemaking School of Social Work
University of Minnesota
1404 Gortner Ave
105 Peters Hall
St. Paul, MN 55108-6160
Phone: (612) 624-4923
Fax: (612) 624-3744
http://ssw.che.umn.edu/rjp

The International Institute for Restorative Practices
P.O. Box 229
Bethlehem, PA 18016
Phone: (610) 807-9221
Fax: (610) 807-0423
http://www.iirp.org

Restorative Justice Community provides an "Electronic Meeting Place" for sharing the many resources developed by the faith community, the nonprofit organizations, and the local, state and federal governmental agencies, in an interactive and productive manner, to help restore and reconcile those impacted by our justice system.
www.restorativejusticecommunity.org

Victim Offender Reconciliation Program of the Central Valley, Inc. (VORP) (Serves victims and offenders of juvenile crime.)
4882 E. Townsend Avenue
Fresno, CA 93727
Phone: (559) 455-9803
Fax: (559) 252-4800
http://vorp.org/index.html

ARTICLES, BOOKS, AND VIDEOS ON COMMUNITY RESTORATION

Blanco, David and Ramsey Alwin. "Examining Prisoner Re-Entry and the CCA Response." Community Services Programs. Center for Community Action Research, 2003. http://www.ezlistings.com/MemberFiles/L1291/Prisoners.PDF

Braithwaite, John. *Crime, Shame and Reintegration.* Cambridge University Press, 1989.

Clear, Todd R. and Karp, David R. "Toward the ideal of community justice." *National Institute of Justice Journal.* Oct. 2000, p.20-8, chart(s), il(s). (Defines and describes this approach to criminal justice, including its focus on restoring what was lost to the victim and community, citizen participation, problem solving, crime prevention, informal social control; U.S., chiefly. This approach is localized and flexible rather than centralized and standardized.)

McGarrell, Edmund F., ed.; and others. *Returning justice to the community: the Indianapolis juvenile restorative justice experiment.* Hudson Institute, Inc., June 2000, bible(s); table(s); chart(s). (Describes implementation and early results on use of Restorative Justice conferences between victim and offender as an alternative response to early law breaking by youth 14 years old and younger with no prior court adjudications. Published by the Crime Control Policy Center.)
http://www.hudson.org/files/publications/Restoring_Justice _Report.pdf

"Senior Ex-Offenders were awarded Certificates of Honor." Senior Ex-Offender Program. (Ex-offenders give back to the community and are recognized for their efforts.)
http://www.gibbsmagazine.com/Ex%20offenders%20award ed.htm

Van Ness, Daniel W. and Karen Heetderks Strong. *Restoring Justice*, second edition. Cincinnati, OH: Anderson Publishing, 2002.

Zehr, Howard *The Little Book of Restorative Justice.* Good Books, 2002.

PROGRAMS AND RESOURCES FOR RESTORATION OF VOTING RIGHTS

Brennan Center for Justice
161 Avenue of the Americas, 12th Floor
New York, NY 10013
Phone: (212) 998-6730
Fax: (212) 995-4550
www.brennancenter.org

Center for Voting and Democracy
6930 Carroll Avenue, Suite 901
Tacoma Park, MD 20912
Phone: (301) 270-4616
http://www.fairvote.org/vra/ex_offender_rights.htm
See Ex-offender Voting Rights
http://www.fairvote.org/vra/ ex_offender_rights.htm

Democracy Works
An Advocacy Center for Democratic Values
44 Capitol Avenue, Suite 102
Hartford, CT 06106
Phone: (860) 727-1157
Fax: (860) 727-1089
www.democracyworksct.org

Demos
220 Fifth Avenue, 5th Floor
New York, NY 10001
Phone: (212) 633-1405
Fax: (212) 633-2015
www.demos-usa.org

Ex-Offenders Voting Rights Act of 2003. H.R. 1433 is a Bill introduced by Rep. Rangel March 25, 2003 to secure the Federal voting rights of certain qualified ex-offenders who have served their sentences.
http://www.theorator.com/bills108/hr1433.html

The Legal Action Center has several publications for assisting returning offenders, including papers on housing, jobs and public assistance.
http://www.lac.org/pubs/gratis.html

"Responsibility, Rehabilitation, and Restoration: A Catholic Perspective on Crime and Criminal Justice." A Statement of the Catholic Bishops of the United States.
http://www.usccb.org/sdwp/criminal.htm

The Right to Vote (hosted by the Brennan Center) campaign has just launched its new website on felony disenfranchisement. Right to Vote is a national collaboration of eight leading civil rights and civil liberties organizations dedicated to removing barriers to voting for citizens with felony convictions. The campaign is engaged in advocacy work at the national level and in targeted organizing campaigns in five states. The new website is a source of information, advocacy, and technical assistance for communities engaged in reform work in this area.
www.righttovote.org

"Rutgers Law School and ACLU Challenge Denial of Voting Rights in Groundbreaking Lawsuit." ACLU, 6 January 2004.
http://www.aclu.org/VotingRights/VotingRights.cfm?ID=14681&c=32

The Urban Institute
2100 M Street, NW
Washington, DC 20037
Phone: (202) 833-7200
www.urban.org

Uggen, Christopher, Manza, Jeff, Thompson, Melissa, Wakefield, Sara. "Impact of Recent Legal Changes in Felon voting Rights in Five States." University of Minnesota Department of Sociology.

Voting Rights Restoration: *2004 Policy Toolkit from the Center for Policy Alternatives* http://www.stateaction.org/2004agenda/50.pdf

About the Author

Pat Nolan is the President of Justice Fellowship, the criminal justice reform arm of Prison Fellowship, founded by Chuck Colson. Justice Fellowship works to reform the criminal justice system based on the principles of restorative justice found in the Bible. Staff work with government officials to find practical ways to apply restorative justice to help victims, reform the hearts of offenders, and restore a sense of community to neighborhoods long plagued by crime. Justice Fellowship advocates that low-risk offenders be sentenced to restitution and community service instead of prison, so they can remain with their families while repaying their victims. JF also promotes programs for reconciliation between victims and offenders, meaningful work programs in prisons, and giving victims explicit rights in criminal proceedings.

Pat brings a unique background to Justice Fellowship. He served for 15 years in the California State Assembly, four of those as the Assembly Republican Leader. He was a leader on crime issues, particularly in behalf of victims' rights. Pat was one of the original sponsors of the Victims' Bill of Rights (Proposition 15) and was awarded the "Victims Advocate Award" by Parents of Murdered Children. He was named Legislator of the Year by many groups, including the AmVets for his work in behalf of Vietnam veterans.

Pat was targeted for prosecution for a campaign contribution his campaign received. The contribution turned out to be part of an FBI sting. He pleaded guilty to one count of racketeering. He served 25 months in a federal prison and four months in a halfway house.

Before Pat entered prison, a friend told him that "for centuries Christians have left their day-to-day world, humbled themselves, done menial labor, prayed and studied their faith. We call that a monastery. View this time as your monastic experience." Pat credits this friend with helping him enter prison in a frame of mind which allowed him to put the time to good use. Pat says he drew great comfort from the story of Joseph in Genesis. "Man intended it for evil, but God intended it for good."

Pat is a much sought after speaker on issues of justice and faith. He was selected by Governor Geringer of Wyoming to be the speaker at his annual prayer breakfast in 2002, and has testified on several occasions before congressional committees on prison work programs, juvenile justice, and religious freedom. He has also lectured at judicial conferences and legal conventions. His opinion pieces have appeared in numerous periodicals including the *Los Angeles Times*, the *National Law Journal,* and the *Washington Times*. He is a frequent guest on talk shows, including "Hannity and Colmes," "Fox Network News," Michael Reagan and Ollie North.

Pat has been appointed to the nine-member U.S. Prison Rape Elimination Commission by the Speaker of the House of Representatives, Dennis Hastert. Justice Fellowship worked very hard to pass the legislation that established the commission.

Pat is the sixth of nine children, and was born and raised in Southern California. He earned both his Bachelor of Arts in Political Science and his Juris Doctorate at the University of Southern California. He also rode as Tommy Trojan,

USC's mascot in the 1974 Rose Parade. Pat and his wife, Gail, have three children: Courtney, 15; Katie, 14 and Jamie, 10. The Nolans live in Leesburg, Virginia, and are members of the St. John the Apostle Parish.

PRISON FELLOWSHIP.

Founded in 1976 by Chuck Colson, Prison Fellowship partners with local churches across the country to minister, in the name of Jesus, to a group society often scorns and neglects: prisoners, ex-prisoners, and their families.

For information about how you can join with Prison Fellowship in:

- Reaching out to prisoners and ex-prisoners
- Assisting families and children of prisoners
- Advocating criminal justice reform
- Promoting Christian worldview (teaching others to live and look at life from a biblical perspective)

Please contact us at the following address:

PRISON FELLOWSHIP • P.O. Box 1550, Merrifield, VA 22116-1550

www.prisonfellowship.org • Phone: **703-478-0100** • Toll-free: **877-478-0100**

GN0408000   000-4026

....

ANGEL TREE.

A Ministry of Prison Fellowship

Breaking the cycle of crime by sharing the love of Christ with children of inmates.

Prison Fellowship's **ANGEL TREE**® helps local churches reach out to the children of prisoners through:

- Gift-giving at Christmas time
- Summer camping opportunities
- Mentoring relationships

Share in welcoming prisoners' children in Jesus' name. Contact us at:

Phone: **1-800-55-ANGEL** • E-mail: **angel_tree@pfm.org**

AT0416000   070-4026

WITH Chuck Colson

B reakPoint provides a Christian perspective on today's news and trends via radio, interactive media, and print.

For more information on Christian worldview, visit BreakPoint's website at **www.breakpoint.org** or call **1-877-3CALLBP** (1-877-322-5527).

- Subscribe to **BreakPoint daily commentaries** (via our website), a free daily e-mail transcript of Chuck Colson's radio commentary offering a Christian perspective on today's news and trends.

- Subscribe to *BreakPoint WorldView* magazine, featuring Chuck Colson's commentaries as well as feature articles to equip readers with a biblical perspective on a variety of issues and topics, by filling in the form below, calling, or visiting our website.

JUSTICE FELLOWSHIP.

J ustice Fellowship, a division of Prison Fellowship, is an online community of Christians working to reform the criminal justice system.

For the latest developments on prisoner reentry and criminal justice reforms, visit Justice Fellowship's website at **www.justicefellowship.org**, or call us at **800-217-2743**.

Subscribe (via our website) to the *Justice eReport*, a free weekly e-mail update on the latest news, research, legislation, innovations, and commentary on reentry and criminal justice reforms.

❏ **Please send me more information on JUSTICE FELLOWSHIP.**

Name _____
(PLEASE PRINT)

Address _____

City _____ State _____ Zip _____

Phone _____ E-mail _____

Church Denomination (optional) _____

If you work in the criminal justice system:

Agency _____ Title _____

MAIL THIS FORM TO: **JUSTICE FELLOWSHIP**, P.O. Box 1550, Merrifield, VA 22116-1550

JF0402000   095-4026